DIGITAL AUDIO PROJECTS

Other Titles of Interest

DIGITAL AUDIO PROJECTS

by
R. A. PENFOLD

**BERNARD BABANI (publishing) LTD
THE GRAMPIANS
SHEPHERDS BUSH ROAD
LONDON W6 7NF
ENGLAND**

Please Note

Although every care has been taken with the production of this book to ensure that any projects, designs, modifications and/or programs etc. contained herewith, operate in a correct and safe manner and also that any components specified are normally available in Great Britain, the Publishers do not accept responsibility in any way for the failure, including fault in design, of any project, design, modification or program to work correctly, or to cause damage to any other equipment that it may be connected to or used in conjunction with, or in respect of any other damage or injury that may be so caused, nor do the Publishers accept responsibility in any way for the failure to obtain specified components.

Notice is also given that if equipment that is still under warranty is modified in any way or used or connected with home-built equipment then that warranty may be void.

© 1989 BERNARD BABANI (publishing) LTD

First Published — May 1989

British Library Cataloguing in Publication Data:
Penfold, R. A.
    Digital audio projects
    1. Digital sound recording & reproduction equipment
    I. Title
    621.389'3

ISBN 0 85934 190 9

Printed and Bound in Great Britain by Cox & Wyman Ltd, Reading

Preface

Digital electronics seems to have been taking over every aspect of electronics over about the last twenty years. Although widely predicted to largely oust analogue electronics in the audio field ten to fifteen years ago, it is really only quite recently that equipment such as digital hi-fi units and musical effects units have been produced and sold in large numbers. The digital revolution has now arrived though, and digital audio is part of everyday life in millions of households.

It has to be admitted that some types of digital audio equipment are probably not practical propositions for the do-it-yourself electronics enthusiast. Compact disc player and digital tape recording projects for the electronics hobbyist do not seem likely in the near future (if ever). On the other hand, there are some relatively simple types of digital audio equipment that fall well within the capabilities of the average electronics enthusiast. These include such things as test equipment, delay lines, and musical effects units.

This book is divided into two sections, with the first covering the basic theory of digital audio. The second section contains some tried and tested circuits for constructors to build, or for experimentation purposes. By current standards the circuits are not highly complex, but they are beyond the scope of complete beginners to electronics construction. However, for someone with a moderate amount of experience they represent some useful and extremely interesting projects to build.

R. A. Penfold

Contents

Chapter 1

BASICS OF DIGITAL AUDIO

Although virtually unknown and unused not so many years ago, digital audio is now very much a part of everyday life. It is rapidly becoming dominant in the fields of hi-fi, telecommunications, and electronic music instruments. While digital systems tend to be substantially more complex than their analogue counterparts, they have definite advantages in terms of performance and facilities. In fact there are some facilities that can be provided in digital audio systems without too much difficulty, but which would be nearly impossible to achieve by purely analogue means. In terms of performance, good digital systems are substantially superior to good analogue circuits. Digital systems almost invariably need some analogue circuitry at their input and output, and in many cases it is difficult to produce analogue circuits that can live up to the quality of the main digital part of the unit.

For the electronics hobbyist there have not been a great many digital audio projects to choose from. Being realistic about matters, a lot of digital audio devices are beyond the scope of the project builder. Maybe a do-it-yourself compact disc player will appear one day, but this type of thing seems unlikely at present. On the other hand, there are some types of digital audio project that are within the scope of electronic project builders. These mainly involve projects based on digital delay lines, such as echo and reverberation units.

In this first chapter we will look at the basic principles involved in converting an audio signal into digital form and then converting it back to an analogue signal again. We will also consider a few practical applications for digital audio circuits. The next chapter deals with practical circuits that are primarily intended for the constructor to adapt and experiment with, but which are tried and tested designs that can be used "as-is" if preferred.

Analogue and Digital
In order to understand the way in which digital audio circuits

1

function you must have a clear understanding of the difference between analogue and digital quantities. Analogue quantities present no real difficulty, as we are dealing with them in real-world situations every day. Weights and distances are analogue quantities, and as such can have any value. In practice there are always limitations on the accuracy with which anything can be measured, but these are due to limitations of the measuring equipment not limitations on the items being measured. With analogue systems the restrictions on accuracy tend to be rather vaguely defined. With (say) a set of scales of the type which have a pointer, the confines on the accuracy of the scales are as much defined by the precision with which you can read the value being pointed to as they are by any basic inaccuracies in the scales themselves.

Digital systems are very different in that they deal in definite values, and have very rigid limitations on their accuracy. If we again take scales as an example, there are now electronic digital scales available, and the set I have produce a readout in grams. There is no difficulty in reading the weight of anything placed on the scales – the weight in grams is clearly shown on the display. Or is it? Even assuming the scale has optimum accuracy, the value on its display is the weight to the nearest gram. Under worst case conditions, a weight of so many and a half grams will be displayed with an error of half a gram. With an analogue display, if a reading is half-way between one scale division and the next, this will be reflected in the position of the pointer. How accurately the scale can be read is to some extent dependent on the skill of the user.

In order to compensate for this lack of precision in a digital display it is necessary to have a multi-digit type. For example, in our example of a scale that displays weights in grams, this is fine for most purposes if weights from something like 100 to 1000 grams will have to be measured. The half gram maximum error then represents in percentage terms an error range of just +0.5% to −0.5% at most. Few analogue displays can be read with this sort of accuracy. On the other hand, if weights of around 1 to 10 grams were to be weighed using this type of scale, the half gram maximum error would represent a percentage error of between 5% and 50%!

Digital systems can work very well, and can be superior to analogue systems, but only if they have sufficient resolution. Many digital devices have what seems to be severe "overkill" when first looking at their specifications. In truth, some digital instruments have more digits than the specification of the circuit driving the display can really justify. However, in many cases the apparent "overkill" is necessary to make up for the inability to provide any analogue style reading between scale divisions.

Binary

When you use an item of digital electronics, such as a calculator or a watch, any numeric data is entered into the unit and displayed in ordinary decimal form. However, the digital circuits do not work directly in decimal numbers. All the data processing is normally done on the data while it is in binary form. Circuits within the unit convert any decimal data you enter into binary form, and further circuits make the conversion back to decimal again so that any data displayed by the system is in a form that you can easily understand. This may seem like doing things the hard way, which in a way it is, but it is not easy to produce electronic circuits that can handle decimal data directly. By contrast, circuits which can handle binary data are very easy to produce indeed. With current technology this decimal-to-binary-to-decimal approach is the only practical one.

The binary numbering system can be a little confusing at first, but really it is more simple and logical than the decimal system. Although binary tends to be regarded as something that has only been put to practical use in relatively recent times, it is in fact a very old numbering system (possibly the oldest of all). Thousands of years ago some ancient civilisations used what was a true binary system as the basis of their weights and measures. Goods were weighed using balance type scales, with a range of weights from minute ones for measuring expensive materials such as gold, through to very large and heavy ones for weighing less valuable goods. Each weight was half as heavy as the next up in the range. This made it possible to weigh out any quantity that was an exact multiple of the basic weight. As a couple of examples, in order to weigh out 9 units, weights 1 and 8 would have been used, or to weigh out 27 units weights 16, 8, 2, and 1 would have been used.

This may all seem to be a long way from modern digital electronic circuits, but both are binary systems that are based on exactly the same principles. In our weights example, the system works perfectly well provided the minimum weight is small enough so that the system has sufficient resolution, just like a digital system. In the two examples given above the weights were given in decimal numbers, and the weights were identified by their weights in decimal units. However, the system could be more accurately viewed in pure binary terms.

The way in which binary numbering operates is very easy to understand, and the most important point to realise is that the only two single digit numbers that can be used are 0 and 1. This makes the system well suited to use with simple logic circuits where these two numbers are represented by a low voltage (about 0 to 2 volts) to represent a 0, or a higher voltage (about 3 to 5 volts) to represent a 1. These signal levels are usually referred to as "logic 0" and "logic 1", or just "low" and "high" respectively. In one of the previous examples I stated that a weight of 27 units would be represented by weights having values of 16, 8, 2, and 1 unit. Looking at things in purely binary terms the weight would be expressed as 11011 units, or the example of 9 units would be 1001 in binary.

In the decimal numbering system the columns represent (working from right to left) the units, tens, hundreds, thousands, etc. In binary they represent the units, twos, fours, eights, sixteens, etc. Thus 1001 in binary is equal to one unit, no twos, no fours, and one eight, and is the equivalent of 9 in decimal. As another example, 11001 in binary is equal to one unit, no twos or fours, one eight, and one sixteen, or 25 in other words $(1 + 0 + 0 + 8 + 16 = 25)$. The way in which electronic circuits handle problems such as decimal points, negative numbers, and calculations is a relatively involved subject. Fortunately, it is not really something that you need to understand in order to master the basics of digital audio. This "direct binary" as it is termed, is all you really need to deal in.

Bits and Bytes

A binary digit is normally termed a "bit", which is merely a contraction of "binary digit". Bits are normally used in blocks of eight bits, or multiples of eight bits, although there are exceptions to this. A group of eight bits are called a "byte", and you may occasionally encounter references to a "nibble". This, believe it or not, is half a byte, or a group of four bits in other words. The bits of a byte are numbered from 0 to 7, with 0 representing the right-most column (the units) and the 7 representing the left-most column. These are often called the "least significant" and "most significant" bits respectively.

The eight bits of a byte enable integers from 0 to 255 to be handled, which is adequate for some purposes but inadequate for many others. It is, of course, possible to use any number of bits together to represent any number you like. Most non eight bit systems use sixteen bits, giving a number range (in decimal terms) of 0 to 65535. A group of sixteen bits is called a "word", but this is not a rigidly defined term, and this name is sometimes used to describe a different number of bits. In particular, in digital audio there are some 12 and 14 bit systems, and groups of 12 or 14 bits are often referred to as a "word". A few systems (but as yet, not digital audio types) use 32 bits of data. A group of 32 bits is normally termed a "long word".

Audio Conversion

The basis of any digital audio system are the analogue to digital and digital to analogue converters. The sound waves that must be digitally processed in some way are converted to a varying electrical signal by a microphone. This signal, usually after some amplification, must then be converted to an apposite digital value. This is the function of the analogue to digital converter. For an eight bit system this means converting the input voltage to a number in the range 0 to 255, and a typical eight bit converter would have an input voltage range of 0 to 2.55 volts. The input amplifier would therefore bring the input signal to a level that would stay within this 0 to 2.55 volt range, but would go close to the limits on signal peaks.

It is important with any audio system that the signal levels are correct so that something approaching the maximum possible signal to noise ratio is achieved. An excessive signal level must be avoided as it will produce clipping. This is where the input signal, in order to produce accurate digitising, would require a value above 255 or below 0. Of course, this can not be achieved by an eight bit system, and so the converter simply produces its maximum or minimum value, as appropriate. This gives a clipped and badly distorted waveform, as demonstrated by Figure 1.1. On most types of signal this type of distortion sounds as what could only be described as pretty terrible.

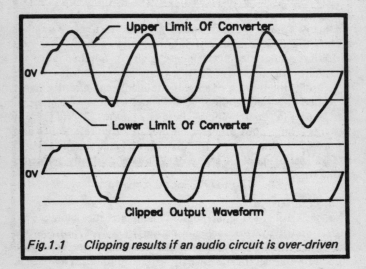

Fig.1.1   Clipping results if an audio circuit is over-driven

Some converters produce an even worse type of clipping (sometimes referred to as "digital clipping"). This is where an input that tries to take the converter beyond its maximum value causes the output to cycle right back to zero, and then increment from there. In other words, an input that required a value of 256 would actually produce an output of zero, one that required a value of 257 would actually produce an output of 1, and so on. This produces an almost instant

6

transition from maximum output voltage to the minimum output voltage as the clipping threshold is exceeded. As the signal passes back below the clipping level the output makes the reverse transition, and almost instantly jumps from minimum value to the maximum one. This is about the worst type of distortion that can occur, and must be avoided if at all possible. Figure 1.2 shows the effect this type of clipping has

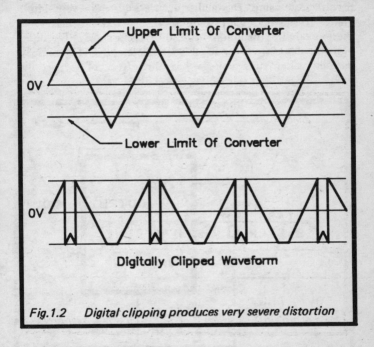

Fig.1.2 *Digital clipping produces very severe distortion*

on the output signal. With a converter that is prone to this cycling back to zero when overloaded, it is normal to include a clipping circuit ahead of it in order to prevent its input voltage exceeding the clipping level. Excessive input levels will then only produce normal clipping, if "only" is a suitable term for the audible effects of hard clipping!

So far we have ignored a slight complication in that the signal from a microphone is an a.c. type. It therefore has alternate peaks of positive and negative voltage. Most analogue to digital converters can not handle negative voltages, and must always be fed with positive input signals. This is not really a major problem since an ordinary converter can be made to handle a.c. signals successfully using some very minor circuitry. A couple of resistors are used to bias the input for a mid-value under quiescent conditions. Most converters have a reference voltage output which provides a potential equal to the full scale value. This makes accurate biasing a very simple matter. The half scale value is 127.5, and the bias value therefore has to be a compromise of 127 or 128. The input signal is capacitively coupled to the converter (Figure 1.3), and this alternating voltage has the effect of varying the input voltage either side of its central bias level.

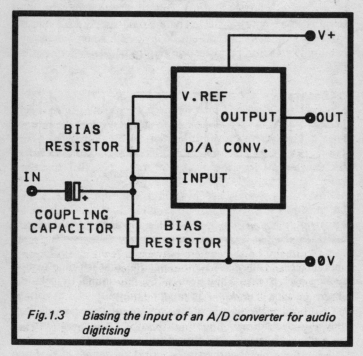

Fig. 1.3   Biasing the input of an A/D converter for audio digitising

This gives the required action with the a.c. input signal being converted to a varying d.c. signal that the analogue to digital converter can process properly. The output from the digital to analogue converter is also a varying d.c. signal, but simply extracting the output signal via a capacitor is sufficient to convert this signal to a true a.c. type.

The digital to analogue converter is usually the more simple of the two converters, and in most cases there is a type available to match whatever analogue to digital converter is used in the system. In our example of an 8 bit analogue to digital converter which can handle inputs in the range 0 to 2.55 volts, the matching digital to analogue converter would have an output voltage range of 0 to 2.55 volts. In fact, it does not matter if the input and output voltage ranges do not match. If the digital to analogue converter had an output voltage range of only 0 to 1 volt, it would still faithfully reproduce the input signal. There would simply be a loss of 6dB or so through the system. Obviously, where necessary, an amplifier or attenuator at the output of the system can be used to make adjustments to the output level.

Resolution
If you start to consider what happens when real signals are fed through a digital recording and playback system, the importance of the system's resolution soon become obvious. If we stay with our eight bit system and its range of 0 to 2.55 volts, this equates to 10 millivolts (0.01 volts) per bit. In other words, input voltages of 0, 10 millivolts, 20 millivolts, 30 millivolts, etc., would be converted to values of 0, 1, 2, 3, etc. A digitising system operates by sampling the input voltage at regular intervals, and in the case of audio digitising the sampling takes place at quite frequent intervals. The sampling rate would normally be somewhere between a few thousand times per second and about 50 thousand times per second. The significance of the sampling rate on the audio quality is something we will consider in detail later on.

Obviously the input signal is not going to conveniently fall at voltages which are exact multiples of 10 millivolts. The converter will simply select the value which offers the best accuracy for each sample voltage, and there will be some error when the signal is converted back to an analogue type. In our example the maximum error is 5 millivolts. A 25.5 millivolt signal for instance, would be converted to a value of 25 or 26, which would give an output voltage of 25 or 26 millivolts from the digital to analogue converter.

On a signal of 2.55 volts peak to peak an error of 5 milli-volts may not seem very significant. After all, it represents only about 0.2% of the converter's full scale value. However, human hearing is very discerning and this error could produce discernable distortion. It is not really distortion on a full 2.55 volt peak to peak signal that is the major problem though.

On a signal that uses the full eight bit range of an analogue-digital-analogue converter system the total harmonic distortion is well under 1%. Although this is less than hi-fi performance, it is still adequate for many purposes. Even if the converters have something less than optimum accuracy, performance should still be ample for many applications. Practical signals almost invariably cover a wide dynamic range, and even if the signal fully drives the converters during peaks of volume, there are likely to be much quieter times when it provides signal levels that are well below the peak levels that the converters can handle.

With a signal at −20dB (i.e. with a voltage of just one-tenth of the maximum level) the converters will only be used over a very restricted range of values. In fact only 25 or 26 different levels would be involved, and any rounding up or rounding down of voltages through the system would be relatively large. Taking things to extremes, at input levels of much less than about −40dB the signal might be inadequate to operate the converter at all, and there would be no output signal!

The basic mathematics of digital distortion are quite easy. Each bit of resolution that is added gives a halving of distortion − each bit of resolution that is removed doubles distortion. As halving the input level is effectively the same as reducing the resolution by one bit, each halving of the signal level is accompanied by doubling of the distortion. In effect the absolute level of the distortion is constant, and so in per-centage terms a halving of the input level gives a doubling of the distortion level. Results may sound quite good at high signal levels where the main signal tends to mask the distortion, but results will be much less good at low signal levels where the main signal is too quiet to mask the distortion properly.

As pointed out previously, low level signals will be lost altogether.

Allied to the distortion problem there is the matter of the signal to noise ratio. With no input signal there may be a constant output level having no significant noise content. Matters are very different when an input signal is present, and there is background noise at a comparable level to the distortion. In practice there may not be a "silent" background with no input signal present, as the converters can tend to alternate between one value and another, generating a random noise background signal. Where possible this should be avoided, especially with systems that do not have particularly high resolution. It can usually be avoided by careful setting up of the bias level, and a sort of built-in noise gate action is then provided.

If we now consider the actual noise and distortion figures obtained with digital audio systems, an 8 bit system has a noise level that can be no better than about $-48dB$, and which could well fall slightly short of this figure in a practical system. This is not really very good, and is comparable to something like a cassette recorder which does not have any form of noise reduction system, or f.m. stereo radio with a slightly inadequate aerial system. The noise will probably be unnoticeable at high signal levels, but will be very intrusive when the signal level is low.

At the maximum input level the harmonic distortion should be under 0.5%, and perfectly acceptable for many purposes. At lower signal levels the distortion level starts to become much more significant though, with a few percent distortion at the $-20dB$ level, and something approaching 50% distortion at $-40dB$. This gives very rough sounding results on low level signals.

Improved Performance
One way to obtain increased performance is to opt for a higher resolution system. With a 12 bit system the noise and distortion levels are 16 times lower than for an 8 bit system. Going up to 16 bit resolution gives a further sixteen-fold improvement in performance, and noise/distortion levels that are some 256 times lower than those of an 8 bit system. Sixteen bit

resolution is used in compact disc players incidentally.

The problem with higher resolution systems for the do-it-yourself enthusiast is that the converter integrated circuits are difficult to obtain, and tend to be very expensive. Discrete component converters are probably not a practical proposition. Methods of gaining improved performance from an 8 bit system probably represent a more practical approach to the problem.

One method is to use special analogue to digital converters that have logarithmic rather than linear scaling. With a linear converter there are equal voltage increments from one converter value to the next. With a logarithmic type the voltage increments are quite small close to the central bias level, and become increasing spread out away from this bias level. This gives fine resolution and relatively good results at low signal levels, but relatively course resolution and high distortion at high signal levels. Instead of having results that rapidly worsen as the signal level is reduced, performance is more consistent over a range of input levels. Performance does still degrade as the input level is reduced, but to a much lesser degree. Although compared to a linear converter the distortion levels are significantly worse at high signal levels, overall noise and distortion performance are much improved.

The signal to noise ratio is very much better at (typically) about −72dB, which is comparable to a lot of hi-fi equipment (but is still something well short of compact disc quality). This gives sufficient dynamic range to ensure that low level signals are not lost altogether. Although it might seem that a lack of linearity in the converters would result in severe distortion through the system, this does not happen. Provided the scaling of the analogue to digital converter is accurately matched by the scaling of the digital to analogue converter, a lack of linearity in the scaling will not introduce distortion.

Companders

Although there is a lot to be said in favour of converters having logarithmic scaling for audio applications, they do not seem to have gained widespread acceptance. They are difficult to obtain, and must be accurately set up if they are to achieve their potential performance figures. Commercial digital audio

12

designers seem to have opted for higher resolution systems based on converters having linear laws. What is possibly a more practical proposition, especially for the electronics hobbyist, is an 8 bit linear system plus a type of circuit called a "compander".

A compander is a form of noise reduction unit, and in one guise or another, units of this type are much used in conventional tape recording. Some offer modest noise reductions of only about 10dB while others offer massive improvements of around 40dB or more. Companding is a double-ended noise reduction system, which merely means it must be used during both the recording process and for playback. A compander is a form of automatic gain control circuit. Audio compression is applied to the input signal, while complementary expansion is applied to the output signal. It is from this compression and expansion that the term "compander" is derived.

During recording, or in the case of a digital processing circuit during the digitising process, the gain is set high on low level signals, but is steadily decreased as the input level is increased. Quite large changes in the dynamic levels are therefore compressed into much smaller changes. A typical compander system uses a 2 to 1 characteristic, which means that (say) a 40dB rise in the signal level would be reduced to an increase of just 20dB after compression. In other words, an increase in level of 100 times at the input would be cut down to a tenfold increase at the output.

The point of using this compression is that it brings low level signals up to much higher levels. Signals that would normally be lost in noise and distortion, or which might fail to activate the analogue to digital converter at all, are brought to a level which is well above the noise and distortion. The obvious problem with compression is that it distorts the signal quite radically by making massive changes in the dynamic levels, and other forms of distortion might also be introduced. This does not matter though, as the expander at the output of the system restores the signal to its former state.

The expander provides the opposite action to the compressor. It provides low gain on low level signals, but provides an increasing amount of gain as the input level is raised. Compressed low level signals that are too high in amplitude are

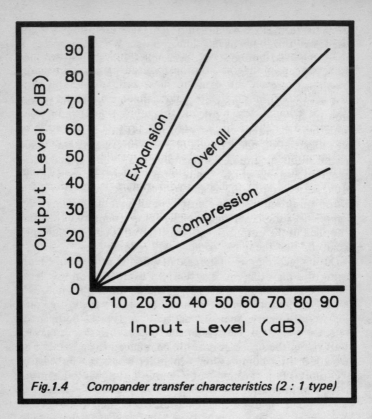

Fig.1.4   Compander transfer characteristics (2 : 1 type)

therefore reduced back to their original levels. Figure 1.4 shows how a compander . changes the recorded signal, but introduces no changes to the dynamic levels of the final output signal.

The background noise and distortion are not affected by the compressor, as they occur in the system at a stage that comes after the compressor. Being low level signals, the noise and distortion are greatly reduced by the expander. In theory, if a system having a signal to noise ratio of −48dB is used in conjunction with 2 to 1 compander unit a 96dB signal to noise ratio is obtained. In other words, an 8 bit system can be given a signal to noise ratio that rivals a 16 bit digital audio system.

In practice things are not quite this simple, and there may be a certain amount of noise introduced by the compander system. However, the signal to noise ratio would still be in excess of 80dB in most cases. Note that a compander system can not combat any noise on the input signal, only noise introduced by the recording/playback process. Any noise on the input signal will be compressed prior to expansion, and will accordingly be reproduced at the normal level.

In my opinion at any rate, the greatest advantage of using a compander with a digital audio system is not the noise reduction it affords, but the reduced distortion levels. If we again assume a compression/expansion characteristic of 2 to 1, the distortion levels on all but the highest level signals are greatly reduced. On a signal at the maximum level there is no improvement as its level is unchanged through either the compressor or the expander. The signal extracts the maximum possible performance from the system without any assistance from the compander.

A signal at −40dB emerges from the compressor at −20dB. As a −40dB signal it would normally be subjected to massive amounts of distortion at something in the region of 25% to 50%. At the compressed level of −20dB this is reduced to a much more modest distortion level of just a few percent. Whereas a −60dB level would normally have no effect at all on an 8 bit digital system, and no output signal would be produced at all, the compressor raises this signal to −30dB. The distortion level is quite high on a signal of this type at something around the 10% mark. However, it is at least reproduced at the output, and is still in a recognisable form. Remember also that a signal at −60dB is very quiet, and the distortion at one-tenth of that level will not be anything like as noticeable as the 10% distortion figure would suggest.

Sampling Rate
As pointed out previously, an audio signal is digitised by sampling the input voltage at regular intervals, with each sample being converted to the appropriate digital value and processed in some way before being converted back to an

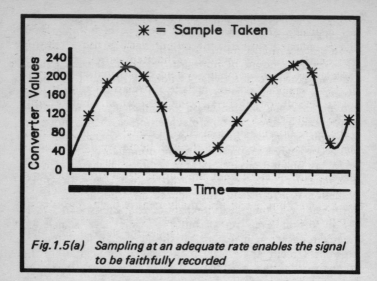

Fig.1.5(a)   Sampling at an adequate rate enables the signal
to be faithfully recorded

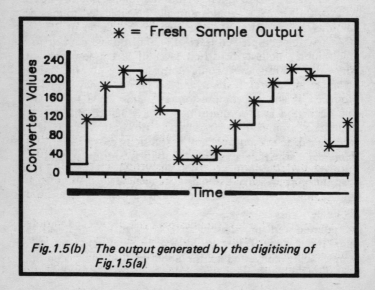

Fig.1.5(b)   The output generated by the digitising of
Fig.1.5(a)

analogue signal. Figure 1.5 helps to explain the way in which this digitising process works, and the type of output signal that is obtained. Clearly the output signal is not a faithful reproduction of the original. The steps are an inevitable consequence of any sampling system, be it digital or analogue. Analogue sampling systems include a lowpass filter at the output to smooth out these steps and recover an accurate copy of the input signal.

Lowpass filtering is also used with digital sampling systems, but its purpose is to remove the high frequency signals caused by the stepping. If left on the output signal these could prevent any unit fed with the output signal from operating properly. This filtering will usually smooth out the steps to some extent, but it will not totally remove them. In order to obtain adequate fidelity it is necessary to have a system which possesses adequate resolution to render the steps so small that the distortion components they introduce are insignificant.

The sampling rate is an important factor, but it is not one that has an affect on the noise and distortion levels. At least, it does not affect the distortion level provided the sampling rate is adequate for the maximum input frequency. It is the maximum usable bandwidth of the system that is governed by the sampling rate. Using a sampling frequency that is too low for the maximum input frequency gives a very severe form of distortion called "aliasing" distortion.

If you consider what happens when an audio signal is digitised, it is not too difficult to see that the sampling rate must be higher than the input frequency. Obviously taking one sample on about every other cycle is not going to give an accurate output signal. As Figure 1.6 demonstrates, you have what is effectively a random voltage generator at an output frequency equal to the sampling frequency. I have always assumed that the term "aliasing" distortion refers to the fact that the output signal assumes a frequency which is equal to the sample frequency, rather than preserving the input frequency.

Clearly at least a few samples per cycle are needed in order to obtain a good quality output signal, but what is the minimum requirement? The theory of sampling systems dictates that the sampling frequency should be at least double the

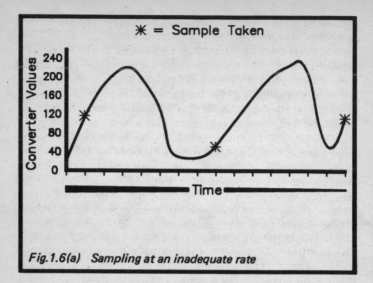

Fig.1.6(a) Sampling at an inadequate rate

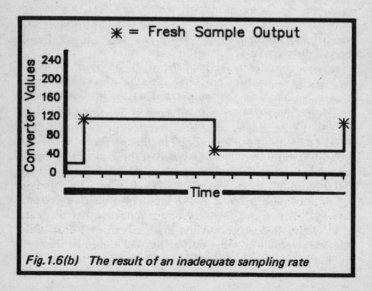

Fig.1.6(b) The result of an inadequate sampling rate

maximum input frequency, and should preferably be three or more times the maximum input frequency.

Note that by input frequency I do not mean the maximum fundamental input frequency. Apart from sinewaves, repetitive waveforms consist of a fundamental frequency plus harmonics (multiples of the fundamental frequency). Even on a fairly low frequency signal it is quite possible for harmonics to extend well towards the upper limit of the audio spectrum. With a sampling rate that is too low to accommodate weak harmonics on the input signal the effect on the output signal is not necessarily too drastic. There may be noticeable distortion products, but the main effect will be a loss of high frequency content on the output signal. With strong input signals at frequencies too close to the sampling rate the result will be very severe distortion indeed.

The upper limit of the audio spectrum is normally accepted as being 20kHz. Therefore, in order to guarantee that an audio signal can be digitised faithfully it is necessary to have a sampling rate of at least 40kHz, and it should preferably be 60kHz or more. Of course, provided less than the full audio bandwidth is acceptable, it is quite in order to use a sampling rate of less than 40kHz. A bandwidth of 10kHz or less will provide results that are adequate for many purposes, and digital audio systems which have a sampling rate of around 20kHz are in common use.

When using low sampling rates there are a few points which must be kept in mind. One of these is to ensure that signals at frequencies of more than twice the sampling rate are not allowed to reach the analogue to digital converter. This would run the risk of aliasing distortion, heterodyne "whistles", and other problems that could degrade the performance of the system. A filter must be used ahead of the analogue to digital converter to ensure that any signals at an excessive frequency are reduced to an insignificant level. It would be standard practice to use a lowpass at the input of a digitising system anyway. This is the only way of guaranteeing that there are no excessive frequencies on the input signal. A lot of audio equipment produces some output beyond the upper limit of the audio spectrum, and there is always the risk of high frequency signals (especially radio signals from powerful broadcast stations) being picked up in the input wiring.

Lowpass filtering would normally be used at the output of a digitising system regardless of its bandwidth. The stepping on the output signal is effectively a squarewave at the sampling frequency added onto the wanted audio signal. Filtering is needed in order to attenuate the resultant high frequencies on the output signal which might otherwise cause problems with the equipment that is fed with the output signal. With a low sampling frequency it becomes very much more important to have really effective output filtering. At sampling rates of about 20kHz or less, the fundamental signal added onto the output signal by the sampling process is at an audio frequency. Without really effective filtering there is a real danger that this will produce an audible tone on the output signal. With low sampling rates it is essential to have really high slope lowpass filtering at the output of the system. Without this filtering either the bandwidth of the system will fall well short of the maximum afforded by the sampling rate in use, or an audible tone will be present on the output signal.

Sample and Hold

With digitising systems that have a sampling rate which is very much higher than the maximum input frequency there are not usually any problems if the input signal, after filtering, is fed straight through to the analogue to digital converter. There may also be no difficulty in doing this if the converter is a very high speed type such as a "flash" converter. In most cases though, either the maximum input frequency will only be about half the sampling rate, and (or) the converter will take a significant amount of time to take each reading. In fact some converters can not make conversions at a fast enough rate for most audio digitising.

A problem that can easily occur is that of the input voltage changing by a significant amount during the course of each conversion being made. Just how this affects results depends on the operating principle of the converter, how long each conversion takes, and similar matters. The result can often be a randomising of the returned values from the converter when there is a strong high frequency content on the input signal. This gives the system a usable bandwidth that is far more restricted than one would expect. The system only works properly at frequencies where little change in the signal voltage occurs during each input cycle, which might be at frequencies of a tenth of the sampling rate or even less!

Clearly some way around this problem is required, as it can massively degrade the performance of a system. The standard approach is to use a sample and hold circuit. This is a circuit that is controlled by a brief pulse, and each time a control pulse is received, the circuit samples the input voltage and maintains that voltage at its output until the next pulse is received and a new sample is taken and stored. In this context things are arranged so that on the trailing edge of the control pulse the analogue to digital converter is triggered, and starts a fresh conversion. This ensures that the converter is fed with a constant voltage during each conversion, and that samples are genuinely taken at regular intervals.

Sample and hold circuits are not particularly complex. They consist basically of an electronic switch, a charge storage capacitor, and a buffer amplifier, connected in the manner shown in Figure 1.7. The control pulse is fed to the control input of the electronic switch, and causes it to close momentarily. While it is closed it charges the capacitor to the input voltage. Once the pulse has ended and the electronic switch has opened again, the capacitor maintains its charge as there is no discharge path for it. I suppose that there is actually a discharge path into the input of the buffer amplifier, but this would normally be based on a f.e.t. input operational amplifier having an input impedance of about 1 million megohms or so. The capacitor is therefore unlikely to discharge significantly even over a period of a few seconds, and is very unlikely to discharge significantly in the 25 nanoseconds or so required for each conversion. Special sample and hold integrated circuits are available, but for most purposes a simple circuit based on an inexpensive CMOS analogue switch plus a MOS input of Bifet operational amplifier will suffice.

The System
If we put together all the points covered so far and apply them to a practical digital processing system, this gives a setup along the lines of Figure 1.8. Here we have a preamplifier at the

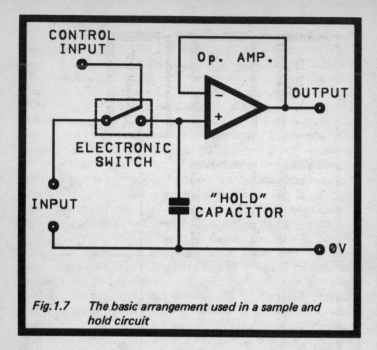

CONTROL
INPUT

Op. AMP.

OUTPUT

−
+

ELECTRONIC
SWITCH

INPUT

"HOLD"
CAPACITOR

ØV

Fig.1.7   The basic arrangement used in a sample and
          hold circuit

input, followed by a lowpass filter and a sample and hold stage. This in turn feeds into the analogue to digital converter's input. The output of the converter is fed into some form of digital processing circuit, which in many cases will be a block of random access memory (RAM). The types of processing and practical applications for digital audio systems is a subject that we will consider very shortly.

On the output side of the system there is just the digital to analogue converter and a lowpass filter. Some form of control logic circuit is needed to ensure that the whole system is properly synchronised. For complex processing a micro-processor controller is needed, but for the more simple applications something very much more basic will normally suffice.

The most basic way of using a digital audio system is to store a short piece of audio which is played back as and when

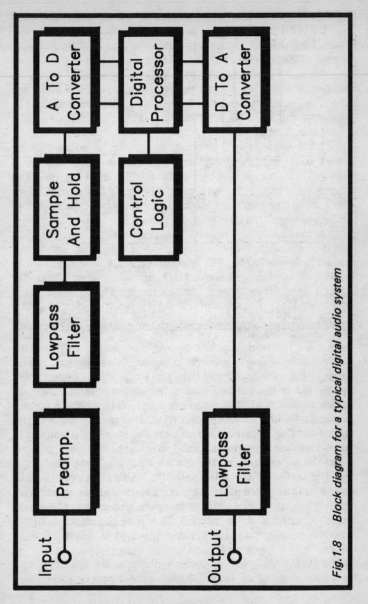

Fig. 1.8   Block diagram for a typical digital audio system

23

required. This type of thing has applications in electronic music, and sound samplers are now very popular instruments. These are mostly quite sophisticated and highly complex pieces of electronics, but even a very basic sound sampler can provide some useful results, especially for percussion synthesis. Sampling is not only used in electronic music, and there are other applications. In particular, short pieces of speech can be digitised and used in applications that require simple speech synthesis capabilities.

Probably the most common use of digital audio systems apart from recording/playback systems is in delay lines. In other words, a circuit where a signal is fed in at one end, and appears out the other end after a certain delay period. This type of circuit is much used in electronic music effects such as echo, reverberation, flanging, chorus, etc.

Like a basic digital recording/playback system, a digital delay line requires the input signal to be digitised and stored in a block of RAM. The amount of RAM used is crucial in both straightforward recording/playback systems and for digital delay lines. For a sampler the length of the sample is controlled by the amount of RAM available. For a digital delay line it is the delay time that is governed by the amount of available RAM. The basic action of a sound sampler is to feed the first sample into the RAM at the first address, the second sample into the second address, the third sample into the third address, and so on. The process stops when either the audio signal to be sampled has finished, or when all the RAM has been used up. The playback process is similar, with the contents of RAM address 1 being fed to the digital to analogue converter, then the data at address 2, then the data at address 3, and so on until the whole sample has been played back.

The action of a digital delay line differs from this in that during the recording process, the circuit does not come to a halt when all the RAM has been used up. Instead, it goes back to address 1 and starts the whole process over again, recording over the data previously stored in RAM. It continues this process indefinitely. However, before each byte (or word) of data is over-written by fresh data, the old data is fed to the digital to analogue converter. Therefore, the input signal is effectively fed through to the output, but a delay is produced. This delay occurs because after each byte is written into memory, the circuit has to write a sample into every other byte of RAM before it comes back to that byte of RAM and outputs it to the digital to analogue converter.

It is not difficult to work out the maximum sample length that can be stored in a given amount of RAM, or the delay time obtained for a certain amount of RAM. A crucial point to bear in mind here is that the maximum sample/delay time is as much dependent on the sampling rate as it is on the amount of RAM available in the system. Dividing the amount of RAM by the sampling frequency in hertz gives the sample length/delay time in seconds. With relatively short times it is easier to have the sample frequency in kilohertz, which then gives the delay/sample period in milliseconds. As a couple of examples, a delay line having 8192 bytes of RAM and a sample frequency of 40kHz would have a delay time of 204.8 milliseconds (8192/40 = 204.8 milliseconds, or 0.2048 seconds). A sampler having 65536 bytes of RAM and a 30kHz sampling rate would have a maximum sample length of approximately 2.184 seconds (65536/30000 = 2.184 seconds).

When making calculations that involve the amount of RAM in a system, bear in mind that 1k of RAM is actually 1024 bytes — not 1000 bytes. Thus 8k is actually 8192 bytes and 64k is 65536 bytes (hence these rather odd figures in our examples above are actually quite likely figures in practice). Of course, the error is quite small if you use 1000 bytes per kilobyte of memory in your calculations, and you may prefer simply to do this and accept the 2.4% error.

At this stage we will not consider the various ways of connecting a digital delay line to obtain the various popular musical effects such as flanging and chorus. This is something which is considered in detail in the section of this book which deals with practical circuits. However, as an example of a digital delay line in action, consider the block diagram of Figure 1.9. This is for an echo unit of the type which produces a single echo. Here the input signal is split two ways, with one part of the signal being taken straight through to the mixer stage at the output, and the other being taken by way of the delay line. Thus the output signal consists of the

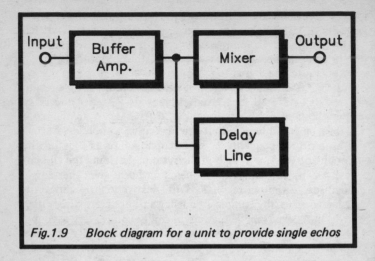

Fig.1.9   *Block diagram for a unit to provide single echos*

straight-through signal and the delayed signal, with the latter
providing the echo.

In order to obtain a proper echo effect the delay line must
provide a delay of at least 60 milliseconds (0.06 seconds). With
a delay of less than this amount but more than about 10 milliseconds (0.01 seconds) this setup will provide a simple chorus
effect. In other words, rather than the delayed signal being
heard as an echo, it will be perceived as a second voice (or
whatever) in unison with the non-delayed one. With analogue
delay lines it can be difficult to obtain a large enough number
of stages to obtain long enough delays for a good echo effect,
and with a large number of stages in use the performance of
the system can leave a lot to be desired (particularly in terms
of noise performance). There is no real problem of this type
with digital systems. Even using a single RAM chip having a
capacity of 8k it is possible to obtain delays of 100 milliseconds or more together with a reasonable bandwidth. The
number of delaying stages has no effect on the reproduction
quality of a digital system. This is governed by factors such
as the system resolution, type of converter used, inclusion or
lack of compression/expansion, etc. One of the great advantages of a digital system is that there is no degradation of the

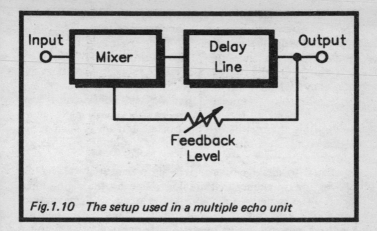

Fig.1.10 *The setup used in a multiple echo unit*

signal while it is in digital form, no matter how long it is stored or how much copying or other processing it undergoes.

Some musical effects units make use of feedback applied over a delay line. The block diagram of Figure 1.10 shows how feedback can be applied to an echo unit to provide a multiple echo of the type that gradually dies away. This basically just involves having a mixer at the input of the unit so that a manually adjustable amount of the output signal can be fed back to the input. With the feedback at maximum the signal is fed back to the input at full strength and it circulates around the system indefinitely. In practice the feedback level would normally be set somewhat lower than this so that there is a small drop in level on each trip through the system. The lower the level of feedback that is used, the quicker the circulating signal decays to an insignificant level.

Converters

There are several types of analogue to digital and digital to analogue converters in common use. Most digital to analogue converters are suitable for audio applications, but not all analogue to digital converter chips are well suited to audio use. Many of these devices are either too slow for audio digitising, or somewhat over-specified and expensive. This second category includes "flash" converters which are intended

27

for video applications and are not really aimed at audio applications. The slow converters are mostly of the counter type, and although they are not much used in audio applications, we will, in due course, study their method of operation. A lot of audio digitising is done using successive approximation converters, and these are really a development of counter type converters. However, first we will consider the basic operation of digital to analogue converters. This may seem to be "putting the cart before the horse", but many analogue to digital converters are built around a digital to analogue converter.

Digital to analogue converters almost invariably make use of electronic switches that are controlled by the digital input signal. The switches are connected into a resistor network of some kind, and this network is sometimes part of the negative feedback network of an operational amplifier. The circuit is usually arranged with a reference voltage providing the input signal to the amplifier, and the resistors/switches connected so that they provide increased gain as more of the digital inputs are taken to the high state. The resistors have values that give a greater increase in gain from the more significant bits than the less significant bits. Thus input 0 can provide double the shift in output voltage provided by input 1, which in turn has half the effect of input 2, and so on, with the desired action being provided.

A lot of digital to analogue converters, including the ones featured in the circuits in this book, use a circuit that is based on an "R − 2R" resistor network. This name is derived from the fact that only two resistor values are used in the circuit, with one of these having double the value of the other. The basic arrangement used in an R − 2R digital to analogue converter is outlined in Figure 1.11.

It would take a lot of mathematics to prove that this arrangement provides exactly the desired action. However, if you are familiar with basic resistor and voltage theory it is not difficult to see that closing a switch has the effect of boosting the output voltage, and that the more significant inputs exercise greater control over the output voltage than do the less significant inputs. If you do some careful calculating you will discover that this arrangement provides exactly the

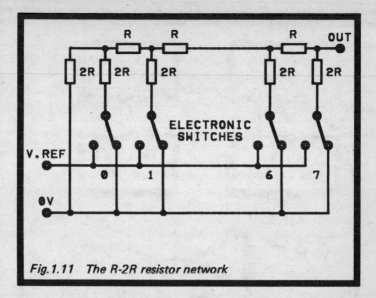

Fig. 1.11   The R-2R resistor network

desired action. The maximum output voltage (i.e. the output voltage obtained with all the inputs at logic 1) is equal to the voltage provided by the reference source.

A/D Conversion

One of the most simple forms of analogue to digital converter is the counter type, and as shown in Figure 1.12, this is based on a binary "up" counter, a high speed voltage comparator, a digital to analogue converter, and a clock generator circuit. At the start of a conversion the counter is reset to zero. Its output is fed to the digital to analogue converter, and so the output of this circuit is also zero. The voltage comparator compares the input voltage with the output of the digital to analogue converter, and while the latter is smaller than the former, the clock generator is allowed to "up" count the binary counter. As the counter is incremented, the output voltage from the digital to analogue converter is stepped higher and higher. Eventually it becomes greater than the input voltage, and the count is then halted. The higher the input voltage, the further the count will progress before it is halted.

29

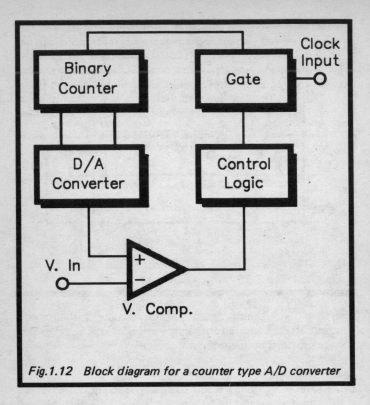

Fig.1.12   Block diagram for a counter type A/D converter

Consequently, this arrangement provides the required action, with the value held in the counter when the count is halted representing an accurately digitised version of the input voltage. The full scale input voltage is equal to the maximum output voltage of the digital to analogue converter circuit.

While this type of converter is capable of very accurate results, it is inherently slow in operation. The number of clock cycles per conversion is not constant. The closer the input voltage is taken to the full scale voltage, the longer it takes for a conversion to be completed. Under worse case conditions, it takes some 256 clock cycles for a conversion to be completed (i.e. when the input voltage is equal to the full scale voltage). Even with a fairly high clock frequency of

1MHz this represents a maximum conversion rate of less than 4000 per second, which is inadequate for most audio digitising. It would provide a bandwidth of only about 2kHz or less.

A successive approximation converter works in a similar manner to a counter type converter, but provides much faster conversions. The arrangement used in a successive approximation converter is shown in Figure 1.13, and this has obvious

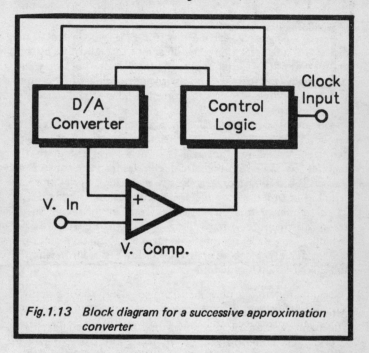

Fig.1.13   Block diagram for a successive approximation converter

similarities to the setup utilized for counter converters. The main difference is that the input signal for the digital to analogue converter is provided by the control logic circuit rather than by a binary "up" counter.

In operation this modified arrangement works in broadly the same manner, and initially the binary code fed to the digital to analogue converter is zero. On the first clock cycle the most significant bit (bit 7) is set high, and the output voltage from the digital to analogue converter is compared with the input voltage. If the input voltage is the higher voltage, bit 7 is left high. If the output potential of the digital to analogue converter is the higher voltage, bit 7 is reset to zero. On the next clock cycle bit 6 is set high, the comparison process is repeated, and bit 6 is left high or reset to zero depending on the result. On subsequent clock pulses the comparison process is repeated for the other bits, working in reverse sequence from bit 5 to bit 0.

As this process is carried out, the binary code fed to the digital to analogue converter becomes, literally bit by bit, an ever more accurate approximation of the correct value, until finally bit 0 is set and an accurate value for the input voltage is provided. It is from this that the "successive approximation" name is derived.

Obviously this method will almost invariably need far fewer clock cycle per conversion than a counter type converter would require, and it is also consistent in that it requires the same number of clock cycles for each conversion. For an 8 bit converter it is usually nine clock cycles that are required in order to complete each conversion. With a 1MHz clock frequency this gives a conversion time of just 9 microseconds, which represents roughly 110000 conversions per second. This is clearly quite adequate for audio digitising, and is considerably more than sufficient for a system having the full 20kHz audio bandwidth.

Alternative Digitising

The basic method of audio digitising described so far is the one in most common use, but there are alternative means of digitising an audio signal. These utilize some form of pulse code modulation (p.c.m.), and of these methods it is probably pulse width modulation (p.w.m.) that is most frequently used. The way in which these systems differ most radically from conventional digitising is that they are single bit systems. Although a conventional digital audio system using single bit resolution would provide massive distortion (as much distortion as wanted signal in fact), pulse code modulation is capable of very high quality results.

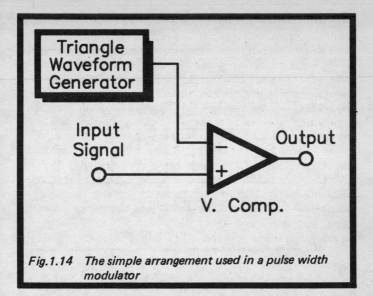

Fig.1.14 *The simple arrangement used in a pulse width modulator*

Pulse width modulation is performed using a setup of the type shown in Figure 1.14. A high speed voltage comparator is at the heart of the system, and this has its non-inverting input fed from an oscillator that provides a triangular clock signal. The clock signal must be at a frequency that is substantially higher than the highest input frequency. The input signal is fed to the inverting input of the voltage comparator. Remember that the output of the comparator goes high when its non-inverting input is at a higher voltage than the inverting input, and low when the comparative input levels are reversed.

If we consider the action of the circuit with the input voltage at the mid-supply level, the clock signal is higher than the input voltage on positive half cycles, but lower than this voltage on negative half cycles. This gives an output voltage that has a 1 to 1 mark-space ratio (a squarewave in other words). The relevant waveforms and their relative timing are shown in Figure 1.15(a). If the input voltage is taken lower, the clock signal is at the higher potential for a greater proportion of the time, so that the output signal becomes a short

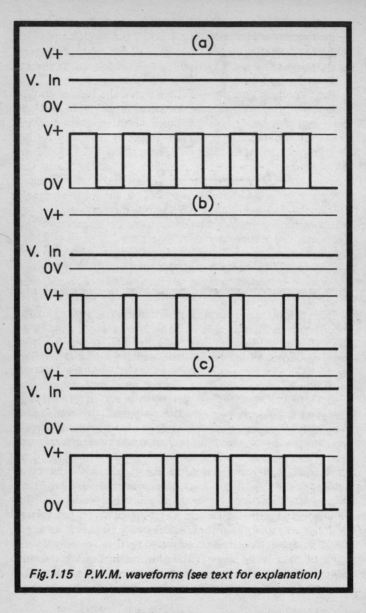

Fig.1.15 P.W.M. waveforms (see text for explanation)

34

pulse type (Figure 1.15(b)). If the input voltage is taken higher than its initial half supply level, the clock signal is at the higher potential for less than 50% of the time. This gives an increased mark-space ratio on the output signal, as shown in Figure 1.15(c).

The important point to note here is that the average output voltage of the pulse signal is the same as the input voltage. Thus, in order to decode the pulse width modulated signal back to an ordinary audio signal it is merely necessary to use some lowpass filtering. This integrates the pulses to produce a high quality audio signal provided, of course, that the encoding process provides good linearity and the lowpass filtering gives a low ripple content on the output signal.

The audio quality of a straightforward encoder/decoder system is almost entirely dependent on the linearity of the pulse width modulator circuit. The situation is very different when the signal is stored in RAM before being retrieved and decoded. There is more than one way of tackling the problem of recording a pulse width modulation signal, but the most simple of these is to sample the state of the signal at regular intervals, and store each sample in a bit of RAM. This system inevitably produces small errors, as the input signal will change state between samples, and this will result in errors on the played-back waveform. These errors will be reflected on the decoded audio signal in the form of distortion.

In order to minimise this distortion a very high sampling rate is required. The higher the sampling frequency, the less room for error that is left on the recorded signal. Although RAM only one bit wide is needed in order to store a pulse width modulation signal, due to the very high sampling rate it does not require any less RAM than a conventional digital audio system of comparable performance. An alternative method of storing a signal of this type is to have a high resolution timer that measures the time between transitions on the pulse signal, with these times being stored in RAM so that the signal can be reconstituted. This requires fewer pieces of data to be stored in RAM, but in order to obtain adequate resolution each piece of data needs to be many bits in length. Whatever system is used, there is always a very definite limit on the performance that can be obtained from a given amount of RAM. The advantage of pulse width modulation is not any saving in the amount of RAM required, it is the simplicity of the decoder circuit. This need consist of nothing more than a few resistors and capacitors, and if taken to extremes a single resistor and capacitor would suffice!

Chapter 2

DIGITAL AUDIO CIRCUITS

Having covered the basic theory of digital audio in the previous chapter, we will now move on to some practical circuits. These are a simple digital oscilloscope store and a delay line which can be used to provide a variety of effects. Both units are based on readily available components that are reasonably inexpensive, and neither cost the relatively large sums of money often associated with digital audio equipment. While these projects are not in the "dead simple" category, they should still be within the capabilities of someone who has a reasonable amount of experience at electronics construction.

Scope Store

An oscilloscope store is a digital circuit that enables an ordinary oscilloscope to effectively operate as a storage oscilloscope. Although most low cost oscilloscopes have a bandwidth of about 20MHz or so these days, a bandwidth as wide as this is impractical for a low cost digital storage unit. It would require D/A and A/D converters having the ability to sample at 40MHz or more. This is about one thousand times the rate at which most low cost A/D converters can operate, and around one hundred times too fast for low cost D/A converters.

This limits a low cost unit of the type featured here to operation over the audio frequency range. This obviously limits the applications of the unit, but it still remains a very useful piece of equipment. Many users only require an oscilloscope for audio frequency use anyway, or this is their main use for the instrument. A scope store is very useful for viewing the waveforms of brief, non-repetitive (or very infrequent) waveforms. It is often necessary in audio work to view brief snatches of signal, and a simple scope store of this type can prove to be invaluable on these occasions.

A unit of this type is a very basic form of digital recording and playback system. The unit operates in the standby mode until it is triggered, and then it records the incoming signal until all its RAM has been used up. The triggering on a unit of this type can be manual, but in most cases it is necessary to resort to some form of automatic triggering. With only quite brief snatches of signal being recorded it is very difficult to get the timing of the triggering sufficiently accurate if it is carried out manually. Triggering becomes very "hit and miss", with more "miss" than "hit". Automatic triggering is usually much more accurate and reliable. This automatic triggering mostly operates by detecting when the input signal has exceeded a certain threshold level.

Once the signal has been recorded and is safely stored in RAM, the next step is to play back the signal into the oscillo-scope. This is basically just a matter of playing back the signal over and over again. The only slight complication is that the oscilloscope must be correctly synchronised with the store unit, so that each sweep of the screen exactly matches up with each playback cycle of the store unit. It may be difficult for the oscilloscope to lock onto the output signal of the scope store correctly — this depends very much on the nature of the signal that has been stored. Normally the scope store unit has a synchronisation output that provides a signal which can be used to synchronise the oscilloscope via its external synchronisation facility.

The basic arrangement used in this scope store unit is shown in the block diagram of Figure 2.1. The analogue to digital converter, digital to analogue converter, and 8 x 8k of static RAM connect together via an 8 bit data bus. The analogue to digital converter is preceded by an amplifier and filter stage. This gives the unit an input sensitivity of about 230 millivolts peak to peak into an impedance of around 300k. There is a volume control style variable attenuator at the input, and the exact input impedance varies somewhat depending on the setting of this control. Only a modest amount of filtering is used at the input of the unit, as it is assumed that the unit will not be fed with signals that have a strong content outside the audio frequency range. Also, any unwanted frequencies on the output signal caused by an interaction between the sampling frequency and a high frequency input signal may be clearly audible on the output signal, but they are unlikely to produce any visible distortion

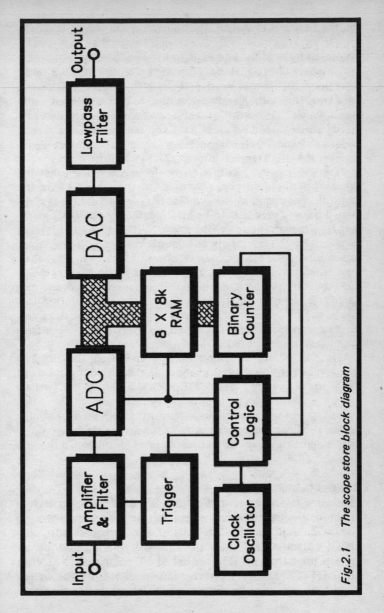

Fig.2.1   The scope store block diagram

on the output waveform. The human ear can almost certainly detect imperfections on sounds much better than they can be displayed by even the highest definition oscilloscope.

Lowpass filtering at the output of the unit is not strictly necessary, as there is no risk of the high frequency components on the output signal causing a malfunction of the oscilloscope. However, a simple single pole filter helps to attenuate any switching noise on the output signal and provides a "cleaner" output signal.

The RAM is stepped through its 8192 addresses by a 13 bit binary counter. This is driven from the clock oscillator by way of the control logic stage. In the record mode the control logic circuit normally holds the binary counter at zero, and does not permit it to be incremented by the clock oscillator. When an input signal above a certain threshold level is detected by the trigger circuit, the control logic block enables operation of the binary counter. However, it only does so for one complete cycle of the counter. After one full cycle of the counter has been completed it is reset to zero and the circuit returns to the standby state. Of course, during this cycle of the counter the control logic circuit provides the necessary control pulses to the converters etc., so that the input samples are stored in the RAM.

Once a full set of samples have been stored, the unit can be switched to the playback mode. In this mode the analogue to digital converter is disabled, the RAM is held in the "write" mode, and the binary counter is cycled indefinitely. The circuit therefore continuously outputs a full set of samples to the oscilloscope. If necessary, a synchronisation signal for the oscilloscope can be extracted from the binary counter.

Control Circuit
The circuit diagram for the control logic, clock oscillator, RAM and binary counter stages of the unit are shown in Figure 2.2. IC1 acts as the basis of the clock oscillator, and this is a standard 555 astable circuit with a variable frequency output provided by VR1. The use of an "improved" 555 such as the TLC555CP is recommended, as these provide better results at the high frequencies involved in this application.

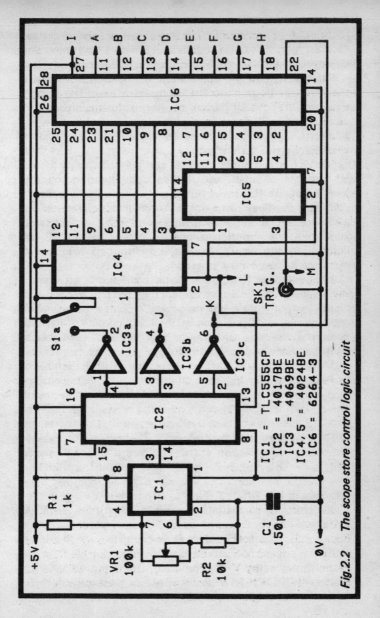

Fig.2.2   The scope store control logic circuit

IC1 = TLC555CP
IC2 = 4017BE
IC3 = 4069BE
IC4,5 = 4024BE
IC6 = 6264-3

41

IC2 is the device at the heart of the control logic block, and this is a CMOS 4017BE decade counter and 1 of 10 decoder. In this case it is the 1 of 10 decoder that is of interest rather than the section of the component that provides a straight-forward divide by ten action. The ten outputs of the decoder are named "0" to "9", and only one of these is high at any one time. Initially, after the device has been reset, it is output "0" that is high. On subsequent clock cycles output "1" goes high, then output "2", and so on, until output "9" goes high. On the next clock cycle the unit returns to its original state with output "0" high, and it then continues the counting action again. In this case I suppose it would be more accurate to describe the device as a one of three decoder, since output "3" is connected to the reset input, and IC2 therefore resets itself when this output goes high. Outputs "4" to "9" are consequently left totally unused, and output "3" only serves to provide this premature resetting.

Output "0" of IC2 is used to activate the "start conversion" input of the analogue to digital converter. IC2 provides positive output pulses, but the required control pulses are all active low types. Consequently, the three outputs of IC2 that are fully utilised are all inverted by CMOS buffers (IC3a to IC3c) in order to provide pulses of the correct polarity.

Output 1 (pin 2) drives the control input of the latches at the input of the digital to analogue converter. This outputs the contents of the current RAM address at this point in each control logic cycle. The RAM contents are read into the digital to analogue converter when the unit is in the record mode as well as during playback. The digital to analogue converter could be suppressed during record, but there would seem to be no point in doing so. Any output from the unit during record can simply be ignored. The control logic cycle is completed by output 2 (pin 4) activating the output buffers of the analogue to digital converter, and setting the RAM device (IC6) to the "read" mode. The value produced by the converter is therefore stored at the current RAM address during this phase of each control logic cycle.

The binary counter is formed by two seven bit counters (IC4 and IC5) connected in series. This gives a fourteen bit address bus, but the fourteenth bit is only used as a synchronisation output for the oscilloscope and to provide a control signal for the trigger circuit. It is worth experimenting a little with different synchronisation outputs, as with some oscilloscopes better results might be obtained using one of the other outputs of IC5 for synchronisation purposes.

Both of the counter chips have their reset terminals controlled by the trigger circuit, and the "inhibit" input of IC2 is controlled by the same source. When in the record mode these terminals are held high, which keeps the counter reset at zero and IC2 inhibited. Once the circuit is triggered these terminals are taken low, and samples are stored in the RAM. This continues until all 8192 RAM addresses have been written to, after which the fourteenth bit of the counter goes high and resets the trigger circuit. The unit is then placed in the standby mode again. When the unit is in the playback mode S1a holds the IC6 in the write mode, and the outputs of IC8 are held in the high impedance state. This prevents the contents of the RAM from being over-written.

A/D Converter

Figure 2.3 shows the circuit diagram for the input filter/amplifier and analogue to digital converter stages. VR2 is the input attenuator, and the output from its wiper is coupled to the amplifier and filter stage by C2. The amplifier is a straight forward operational amplifier non-inverting mode circuit having a nominal voltage gain of 11 times. The filtering is obtained by including C4 in the negative feedback network. R3 and R4 have deliberately been given unequal values so that the biasing of the amplifier has the output at something well below the usual half supply voltage level. This is necessary due to the non-symmetrical output stage of IC7, and the low supply voltage used for this circuit. Normal biasing would result in positive half cycles being severely clipped.

The digital to analogue converter is based on a Ferranti ZN449E successive approximation converter (IC8). The ZN448E and ZN447E chips are identical to the ZN449E, they differ only in price and their guaranteed level of accuracy. The ZN449E is the cheapest and least accurate of the three, but it is perfectly adequate for the present

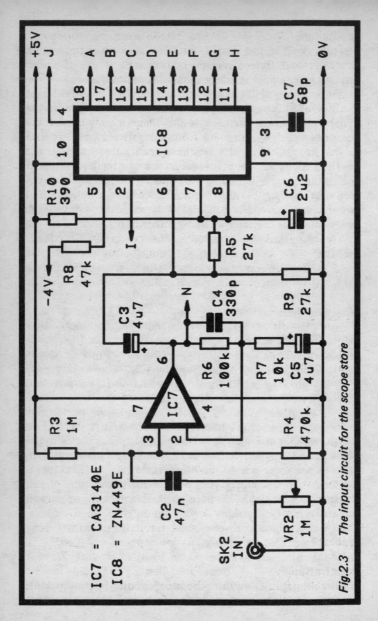

Fig.2.3   The input circuit for the scope store

44

application. The ZN447E and ZN448E will of course work perfectly well in this circuit, but they are substantially more expensive and their increased performance is not likely to produce any noticeable improvement in performance.

Very few discrete components are required in order to get the ZN449E functioning in a practical circuit. R8 is the "tail" resistor for the high speed comparator stage of the converter. This must be fed from a negative supply rail, but as will be explained shortly, this is easily derived from the +5 volt supply rail. The ZN449E contains a high quality 2.55 volt reference voltage generator for its digital to analogue converter section, but this requires discrete load resistor R10 and decoupling capacitor C6. The input of the converter is biased from the reference source by R5 and R9.

The ZN449E has an internal clock oscillator which requires only one external component — a timing capacitor to set the clock frequency. This device is guaranteed to operate with clock frequencies of up to 1MHz, and a timing capacitor of about 82p in value will set this frequency. I have specified a slightly lower value for C7 as in practice ZN449Es seem to be able to operate reliably at clock frequencies substantially higher than 1MHz. It is likely that a value even lower than 68p will be usable, and with some devices satisfactory results seem to be obtained with no timing capacitor! The self-capacitance of the component then sets the clock frequency, usually at something in the region of 2MHz.

It is advisable to use the lowest possible timing capacitance so that the shortest possible conversion time is obtained. This circuit does not incorporate a sample and hold circuit, and in order to obtain good results at higher audio frequencies it is essential to have a short conversion time. The ZN449E is guaranteed to operate reliably with a conversion time of just 9 microseconds, and in practice most devices seem to be well able to achieve something in the region of 5 microseconds. This is short enough to give good results in audio digitising applications.

Negative Supply

A suitable negative supply generator circuit for the ZN449E analogue to digital converter is shown in Figure 2.4. This

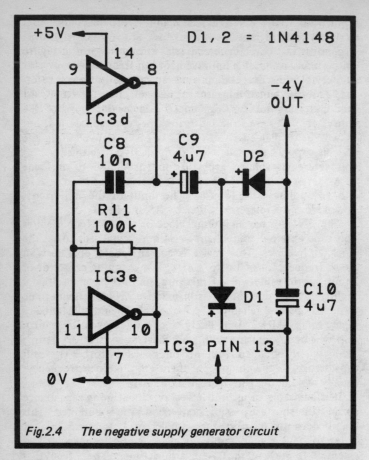

Fig.2.4   The negative supply generator circuit

makes use of two "spare" inverters from IC3. These are
connected in a standard CMOS astable circuit, and the output
from this oscillator is coupled to a simple rectifier and smoothing circuit. The output from this circuit is a d.c. supply of
about −4 volts. The maximum output current from a simple
circuit of this type is very limited, but it is perfectly adequate
for present requirements where a current of only a few tens
of microamps is required. Note that there is a sixth inverter in
IC3. If this is left unused it would be advisable to connect its

46

input (pin 13) to one or other of the supply rails rather than to simply leave it floating.

The digital to analogue converter circuit appears in Figure 2.5. This is based on a Ferranti ZN428E R/2R type converter (IC9). Like the ZN449E, this has an integral 2.55 volt reference source which requires a discrete load resistor and decoupling capacitor (R12 and C12 respectively). It has a

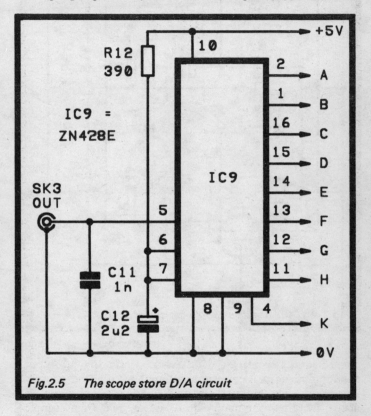

Fig.2.5   The scope store D/A circuit

built-in eight bit latch which is controlled via pin 4. This input is normally high and a negative pulse produces the latching action. As explained previously, in this case the control pulses are generated by IC2 and IC3. The ZN428E has

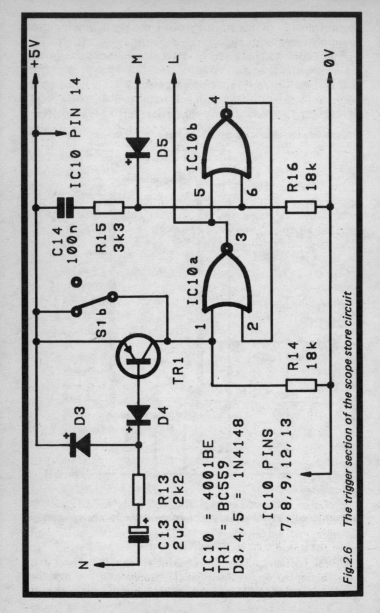

Fig.2.6 The trigger section of the scope store circuit

48

separate digital and analogue ground terminals, but in this circuit they are both simply wired to the 0 volt supply rail. Output filtering is provided by C11 in conjunction with the output impedance of IC9.

The trigger circuit appears in Figure 2.6. It is based on a simple set/reset flip/flop formed from two of the CMOS gates in IC10. The other two gates are left unused incidentally, but their inputs should be connected to one of the supply rails so that they are not left vulnerable to static damage. The flip/flop is initially reset by the pulse it receives from C14 etc. at switch on. It is set when TR1 is switched on, and this occurs when it receives a reasonably strong output signal from the amplifier/filter stage. A simple rectifier circuit based on D3 and D4 ensures that TR1 is operated reliably from the a.c. input signal. The reset signal is coupled to the flip/flop via D5 once a full set of samples has been taken and the output from the fourteenth bit of the binary counter has gone high. As explained previously, the output of the flip/flop is used to control the reset inputs of the binary counter circuit and the "inhibit" input of IC2. S1b holds the flip/flop in the set state when the unit is in the playback mode. This gives continuous operation of the binary counter etc.

Mains PSU

The current consumption of the scope store circuit is quite high at around 90 milliamps, and it could exceed 100 milliamps. This is a bit too high to be easily provided by a battery, although it could be obtained from (say) six HP11 or HP2 size cells fitted in a plastic holder, using a regulator circuit to drop the nominal 9 volt output of the batteries to the required supply potential of 5 volts. A better solution would probably be provided by four HP11 or HP2 size nickel-cadmium cells in a plastic holder (these are the "C" and "D" size nickel-cadmium cells respectively). These provide an output potential of approximately 5 volts, and can therefore be used to power the unit direct.

Unless portable operation is essential for some reason it is much better to use a mains power supply unit. A suitable circuit is provided in Figure 2.7. This is just a standard 5 volt

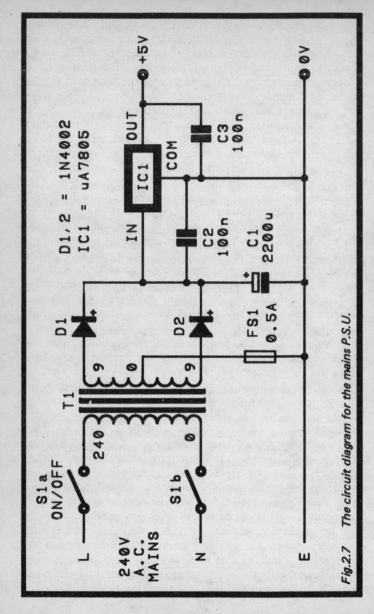

Fig.2.7   The circuit diagram for the mains P.S.U.

50

power supply circuit having full wave (push-pull) rectification and a 5 volt monolithic voltage regulator to give a well smoothed and stabilised output. Note that FS1 should be an anti-surge type, and not an ordinary fuse of the quick-blow variety. A quick-blow fuse is unsuitable for operation in this circuit as it would almost certainly be "blown" by the large surge of current at switch-on as C1 charges up.

The components list specifies a $9 - 0 - 9$ volt transformer for T1. A type having two 9 volt secondaries of suitable current rating should work equally well. The 9 volt terminal of one winding is connected to the 0 volt winding of the other, and these are then effectively the 0 volt centre tap. The remaining 0 volt and 9 volt terminals then act as the 9 volt terminals of the transformer.

If you use a mains power supply circuit for the unit, take due care in its construction, and observe all the normal safety precautions. The unit must be built into a case that has a screw fitting lid or cover so that there is no easy way of gaining access to the dangerous mains wiring. Any exposed metal work must be earthed to the mains earth lead. In practice this is much easier if a case of all metal construction is used. The case is then connected to the mains earth lead, and a soldertag fitted on one of T1's mounting bolts makes a convenient chassis connection point. Any fixing screws etc. fitted on the case will then be in electrical contact with it, and will be connected to the mains earth lead via the case.

Input Amplifier

The input circuit provides a reasonable degree of sensitivity, and the unit can be fed successfully from many signal sources. However, it provides nothing like the sensitivity needed for operation with a microphone to pick up "live" sounds. For microphone operation the preamplifier circuit of Figure 2.8 can be used. This circuit is inevitably very sensitive to stray pick up of electrical signals, and it is a good idea to build it as a totally independent unit with its own power supply (a small 9 volt battery such as a PP3 will suffice). The digital circuits in the scope store unit are very good at generating electrical noise at audio frequencies, and having the preamplifier as a

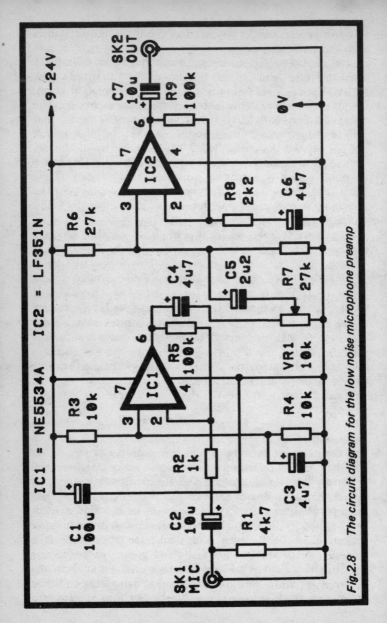

Fig.2.8   The circuit diagram for the low noise microphone preamp

52

separate circuit should ensure that there are no difficulties with excessive noise pick up.

The circuit is a straightforward two stage type having IC1 as an inverting amplifier and IC2 as a non-inverting type. The input impedance of the unit is approximately 800 ohms, which is suitable for most low impedance microphones. The NE5534A specified for IC1 is a very low noise device that gives excellent noise performance despite the high overall voltage gain of the circuit (over 72dB, or some 4500 times). A lower cost device such as an LF351N will work in the IC1 position, but might give a noticeably higher noise level, particularly if the unit is used in conjunction with very low output microphones.

When constructing the preamplifier bear in mind that it has a very high voltage gain, and that due care needs to be taken with the component layout. Avoid leads of more than about 20 millimetres or so in length at the input of the circuit unless they are screened. Keep the input and output wiring as well separated as possible. It is a good idea to house the project in a metal case earthed to the negative supply rail so that the circuit is provided with overall screening from sources of electrical interference. All external leads should be of the screened variety. The current consumption of the circuit is only a few milliamps and a small 9 volt battery such as a PP3 type is perfectly adequate as the power source.

In Use

The basic process of using the scope store is to first set it to the record mode, set VR2 for the correct sensitivity, and then feed in the signal to be recorded. The unit is then set to the playback mode, and the recorded signal is displayed on the screen of the oscilloscope. The output of the unit must, of course, be connected to the Y input of the oscilloscope via a screened lead, and if the trigger output of the unit is to be utilized, this must be coupled to the external synchronisation socket of the oscilloscope. With dual trace oscilloscopes it is sometimes easier to obtain a really stable trace by connecting the trigger output of the scope store to the Y2 input of the oscilloscope, with the main output signal being coupled to the Y1 input. The synchronisation signal can either be displayed but ignored, or the controls of the oscilloscope can be adjusted to set it somewhere off-screen and out of sight.

In practice it might take a few dummy runs in order to get the recording right with VR2 set for the optimum recording level. The oscilloscope might be able to properly synchronise with the output of the store unit using just the internal synchronisation, but in most cases results will be more reliable using the external synchronisation facility or the alternative method described previously. VR1 is used to set the sampling rate, and it is generally best to use the shortest sampling period that gives satisfactory results (i.e. VR1 set for the lowest resistance that gives a sufficiently long recording time).

With relatively low clock frequencies the recording time will be a few hundred milliseconds, and the number of times per second each set of samples is played back will be quite low. Unless the oscilloscope has a long persistence c.r.t. this will give quite a flickery display. Even so, it is very much better than trying to view a short piece of audio signal on a "single shot" basis. However, things can be considerably improved by setting the clock frequency control to maximum so that the recorded signal is played back at the highest possible rate.

Normally the recording and playback rates are the same, and the time scaling on the oscilloscope's X axis is valid on the played back signal. Of course, if the playback rate is speeded up, the X scaling is no longer valid. However, if the oscilloscope's sweep speed is increased so that the full sample is again displayed, then this effectively restores the old X scaling. In other words, if the sweep speed was originally 10 milliseconds per division, but an increase in the playback rate requires it to be increased to 2 milliseconds per division in order to restore the full sample on screen, the effective sweep speed is still 10 milliseconds per division (provided everything is adjusted with suitable accuracy).

The clock frequency can be adjusted from about 75kHz to approximately 300kHz. Bear in mind though, that the sampling rate is one-third of the clock frequency due to the divide by three action of the control logic circuit. The sampling rate is therefore variable from about 25kHz to around the 100kHz mark. In terms of storage time this works out at about 82 milliseconds at the maximum clock rate, and about 328 milliseconds at the minimum clock rate. It might be possible to obtain a higher maximum sampling rate by making C1 lower in value, but this is dependent on the clock frequency of the converter having been optimised at something well in excess of 1MHz.

The minimum clock frequency can be reduced by making C1 higher in value. It is not really feasible to have a sampling rate of much less than 25kHz though, as to do so would restrict the bandwidth of the unit, and the input filter is inadequate. Even with rates of around 25 to 35kHz the unit may not function very well. This depends on the nature of the input signal, and in particular, on the strength of its high frequency content.

Components for Scope Store
(Figs 2.2, 2.3, 2.4, 2.5 and 2.6)

Resistors (all 0.25 watt 5% carbon film unless noted)

R1	1k
R2	10k
R3	1M
R4	470k
R5	27k 1%
R6	100k
R7	10k
R8	47k
R9	27k 1%
R10	390
R11	100k
R12	390
R13	2k2
R14	18k
R15	3k3
R16	18k

Potentiometers

VR1	100k lin
VR2	1M lin

Capacitors

C1	150p polystyrene
C2	47n polyester
C3	4μ7 63V elect
C4	330p ceramic plate
C5	4μ7 63V elect
C6	2μ2 63V elect
C7	68p polystyrene
C8	10n polyester
C9	4μ7 63V elect
C10	4μ7 63V elect
C11	1n polyester
C12	2μ2 63V elect
C13	2μ2 63V elect
C14	100n polyester

Semiconductors

IC1	TLC555CP
IC2	4017BE
IC3	4069BE
IC4	4024BE
IC5	4024BE
IC6	6264-3
IC7	CA3140E
IC8	ZN449E
IC9	ZN428E
IC10	4001BE
TR1	BC559
D1 to D5	1N4148 (5 off)

Miscellaneous

S1	DPDT toggle
SK1	BNC socket
SK2	Standard ¼ inch jack socket
SK3	Standard ¼ inch jack socket

Circuit board, d.i.l. i.c. holders, wire, control knobs, etc.

Note that this circuit uses only relatively slow access times to the RAM, and that any version of the 6264 RAM chip should be perfectly suitable.

Components for Mains Power Supply (Fig. 2.7)

Capacitors
C1	2200µ 16V elect
C2	100n ceramic
C3	100n ceramic

Semiconductors
IC1	µA7805 (1A 5V positive voltage regulator)
D1	1N4002
D2	1N4002

Miscellaneous
FS1	20mm 500mA anti-surge fuse
T1	Mains primary, 9 – 0 – 9 volt 500mA secondary (see text)
S1	Rotary mains switch

20mm fuseholder, mains lead and plug, wire, solder etc.

Components for Preamplifier (Fig. 2.8)

Resistors (all 0.25 watt 5% carbon film)
R1	4k7
R2	1k
R3	10k
R4	10k
R5	100k
R6	27k
R7	27k
R8	2k2
R9	100k

Potentiometer
VR1	10k log

Capacitors
C1	100µ 25V elect
C2	10µ 25V elect
C3	4µ7 63V elect

C4	4μ7 63V elect
C5	2μ2 63V elect
C6	4μ7 63V elect
C7	10μ 25V elect

Semiconductors
| IC1 | NE5534A |
| IC2 | LF351N |

Miscellaneous
| SK1 | Standard ¼ inch jack socket |
| SK2 | Standard ¼ inch jack socket |

Metal case, circuit board, 8 pin d.i.l. i.c. holders, wire, etc.

Digital Delay Line

The digital scope store circuit provides what is almost the required action for a digital delay line. When in the record mode it outputs the contents of each RAM address before recording a fresh sample into that address. Having recorded a full set of samples it then stops until it is set to the playback mode. In order to obtain a delay line action it is merely necessary to have the unit in the record mode, but cycling indefinitely. On the first record cycle the unit outputs noise, since the RAM will not have been recorded into at that stage, and will simply contain random numbers. On subsequent cycles it will output the samples recorded on the previous cycle, thus giving the required delay line action.

In some respects a delay line version of the circuit can be more simple than the original scope store version. The trigger circuit can be totally dispensed with and the control logic section can be slightly simplified as no record/playback switching is required. On the other hand, the input and output filtering needs to be somewhat better than that provided in the scope store unit. Also, the use of a compander is unlikely to give any noticeable improvement in the performance of the scope unit, as few (if any) oscilloscopes provide sufficient screen resolution to merit increased performance (no steps in the waveforms are visible when viewing the output of the unit on my oscilloscope). With a delay line the situation is very different, and the human ear is well able to detect the inadequacies of an eight bit system, especially at low recording levels. A compander is not essential for an eight bit delay line, but I would not use a unit of this type that did not incorporate a reasonably efficient compander.

The delay line described here is very much based on the scope store circuit, and it includes an optional 2 : 1 compander circuit. I would strongly urge the inclusion of this circuit as it really does provide a vast improvement in performance. The signal to noise ratio is improved from around −46dB to about −80dB. As explained in Chapter 1, it is not just the signal to noise ratio that is improved by companding an audio digitising system. The compander effectively provides distortion reduction as well, and the output is very much "cleaner" sounding at low signal levels if this circuit is included in the unit. The use of a noise/distortion reduction system is especially important if the unit is used in an application where some of the output signal is fed back to the input. This tends to recirculate noise around the system and significantly degrades the signal to noise ratio. It is therefore important to have a basic signal to noise ratio that provides sufficient "headroom" to give good results after the increase in the background noise level produced by the introduction of feedback.

Delay Line Circuit

The circuit diagram for the control logic section of the digital delay line appears in Figure 2.9. This is essentially the same as the equivalent circuit in the scope store unit, and the similarities between the two circuits should be readily apparent. The main difference is that the record/playback switch has been omitted, and the analogue to digital converter always writes a sample to RAM each time a RAM address is accessed. The "inhibit" terminal of IC2 is permanently wired to the 0 volt supply rail so that this device is always operational, and the reset inputs of IC4 and IC5 are also connected to the 0 volt supply rail. This means that the counters also operate continuously. In other respects the circuit is no different to the control logic section of the scope store unit.

The analogue to digital converter section of the unit is very similar to the equivalent section of the scope store, and it only

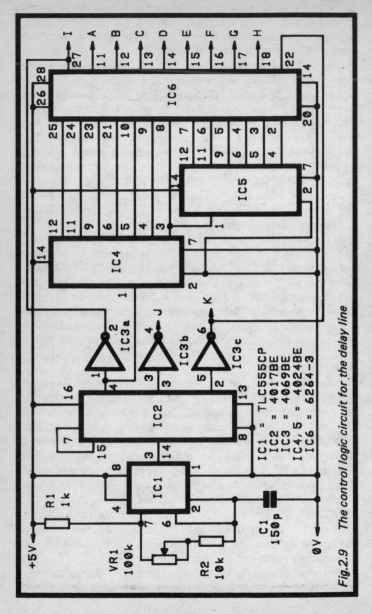

Fig.2.9   The control logic circuit for the delay line

IC1 = TLC555CP
IC2 = 4017BE
IC3 = 4069BE
IC4,5 = 4024BE
IC6 = 6264-3

60

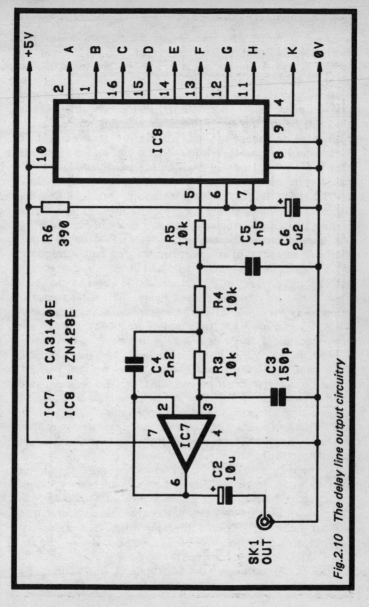

Fig.2.10 The delay line output circuitry

61

differs from it in that a higher quality filter is used at the analogue output. The relevant circuit diagram is shown in Figure 2.10. The filter is a three stage (18dB per octave) type having a cutoff frequency at approximately 20kHz. This filter frequency assumes that the delay line will not be used with very low sample frequencies (by which I mean sample rates of much below about 40kHz). Obviously at frequencies of much below this figure the filter will not provide a very high level of attenuation, and satisfactory results might not be obtained. This depends to a large extent on the equipment that is fed with the delay line's output signal, and how well it can handle any ultrasonic frequencies on the input signal.

The delay line is usable with sample rates of less than 40kHz, but only with some modifications to the output filter. Its cutoff frequency must be no higher than half the sample frequency, and should preferably be something closer to one-third of the sample rate. The cutoff frequency of the filter is easily changed, and it is just a matter of increasing the values of C3, C4, and C5 in order to reduce the cutoff frequency to the desired figure. The filter frequency is inversely proportional to the values of these components. Thus, for example, if a 10kHz cutoff frequency was required, the values of all three capacitors would need to be doubled. Clearly the calculated values are unlikely to exactly coincide with preferred values, but choosing the nearest preferred value should give satisfactory results. If the required value falls almost exactly half way between two preferred values, choose the higher of the two preferred values. This gives less risk of any unwanted peaks in the response, and it is better to have the filter frequency slightly too low rather than slightly too high.

If the unit is to be operated with the sampling rate only two to three times the filter frequency there is a definite advantage in having a filter with a higher attenuation rate. A simple way of achieving this is to have a second filter wired in series with the original. In order words, have a duplicate filter circuit containing IC7, C3, C4, C5, R3, R4, and R5 (but not C2). Disconnect C2 from the original IC7 and connect it instead to the output of the additional IC7. The output of the original filter is then connected to the input (R5) of the

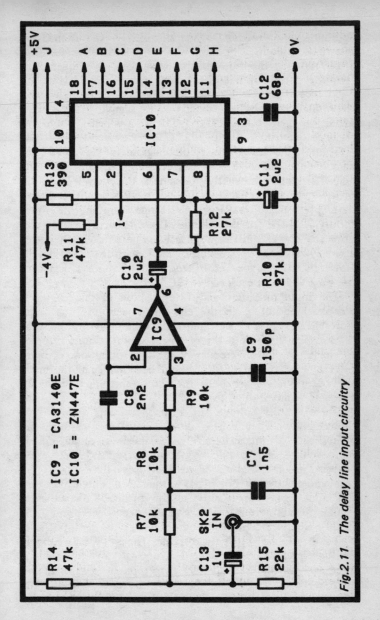

Fig.2.11 The delay line input circuitry

63

additional filter section. This will increase the attenuation rate to some 36dB per octave, which should give over 40dB of attenuation at the fundamental frequency of the sampling frequency, and over 80dB of attenuation at the second harmonic. If necessary more filter stages could be added, and this would certainly be necessary if the sampling rate is made much less than about 20kHz (something which I would not really recommend).

Figure 2.11 shows the circuit diagram for the input filter and analogue to digital converter stages of the unit. The converter section is exactly the same as the equivalent section of the scope store circuit. Actually this is not quite true, as I have specified a ZN449E for the scope store and the higher quality ZN447E for this circuit. There is some advantage in using the ZN447E in this application where its slightly higher accuracy should be reflected in lower distortion levels. However, in practice results seem to be quite satisfactory using a ZN448E or even a ZN449E.

The input amplifier and filter section of this circuit is completely different to the equivalent section of the scope store circuit. It is in fact identical to the delay line's output filter. Like the output filter, if necessary it is quite in order to change the cutoff frequency and (or) to add one or more filter blocks. Good results should be obtained if the input and output filters are both the same (and are both of an adequate standard of course).

There is unity voltage gain through the input and output filters, and as there is also unity voltage gain through the digital part of the system, this obviously gives the circuit unity voltage gain overall. An input level of 2.55 volts peak to peak is needed in order to fully drive the unit. If the compander system is not fitted to the unit it is important that the input signal comes close to this figure. With the compander fitted there is much greater "headroom", and satisfactory results will probably be obtained with the input level well short of 2.55 volts peak to peak. The unit is only suitable for high level signals though. For use with a very low input level, such as that provided by a microphone, a suitable preamplifier must be added ahead of the unit's input. The microphone preamplifier for the scope store unit is also suitable for use with the digital delay line incidentally.

A negative supply is needed for the analogue to digital converter, and this is derived from the +5 volt supply in much the same way as the negative supply was generated for the scope store unit. The relevant circuit diagram appears in Figure 2.12.

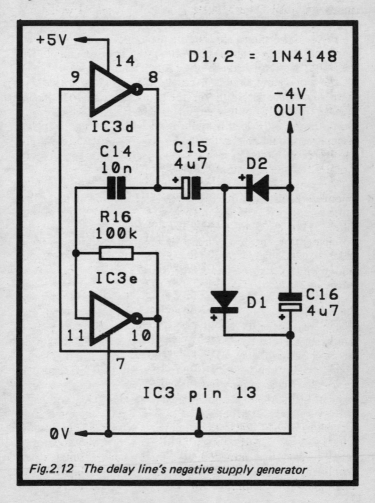

Fig.2.12 The delay line's negative supply generator

Components for Delay Line (Figs 2.9, 2.10, 2.11 and 2.12)

Resistors (all 0.25 watt 5% carbon film unless noted)

R1	1k
R2, R3, R4, R5	10k
R6	390
R7, R8, R9	10k
R10	27k 1%
R11	47k
R12	27k 1%
R13	390
R14	47k
R15	22k
R16	100k

Capacitors

C1	150p polystyrene
C2	10μ 25V elect
C3	150p polystyrene
C4	2n2 polyester
C5	1n5 polyester
C6	2μ2 63V elect
C7	1n5 polyester
C8	2n2 polyester
C9	150p polystyrene
C10	2μ2 63V elect
C11	2μ2 63V elect
C12	68p polystyrene
C13	1μ 63V elect
C14	10n polyester
C15	4μ7 63V elect
C16	4μ7 63V elect

Semiconductors

IC1	TLC555CP
IC2	4017BE
IC3	4069BE
IC4	4024BE

IC5	4024BE
IC6	6264-3
IC7	CA3140E
IC8	ZN428E
IC9	CA3140E
IC10	ZN447E
D1	1N4148
D2	1N4148

Miscellaneous

| SK1 | Standard ¼ inch jack socket |
| SK2 | Standard ¼ inch jack socket |

Circuit board, d.i.l. i.c. holders, wire, etc.

Compander

As pointed out previously, if you want to obtain really good results from a linear 8 bit system it is essential to use a compander to process the input and output signals. Although companders can be quite complex and difficult to set up properly, there is an easy solution to the problem in the form of a special integrated circuit. This is the NE570, which is also available as the NE571. The only difference between these two components is that the NE570 has a slightly higher specification. In particular, it can operate at a slightly higher maximum supply voltage (24 volts as opposed to the 18 volt rating of the NE571), and its guaranteed distortion performance is somewhat superior. Either device can be used in the circuits shown here, but obviously the NE570 with its higher specification is preferable. On the other hand, I found that results were very acceptable using the NE571.

The NE570/NE571 contains two identical sets of electronic building blocks, and these can operate as a compressor or an expander. It is the discrete circuitry that determines the function of each set of blocks. In this case it has been assumed that one section of the device will be used as a compressor at the input of the unit while the other will act as the complementary expander at the output of the circuit. The compression/expansion characteristic is a standard 2 : 1 type incidentally. The basic building blocks of the NE570/

NE571 are a variable gain cell, a precision full wave rectifier, an operational amplifier, and a bias circuit.

When used as a compressor the variable gain cell is connected in the negative feedback circuit of the operational amplifier. The precision rectifier is fed from the output of the amplifier, and it in turn drives the control input of the variable gain cell. As the output level rises, the input voltage to the variable gain cell also rises, and it passes the feedback signal more readily. In other words, it provides increased negative feedback and reduces the voltage gain of the operational amplifier. This gives a decrease in gain as the input level is increased, and applies the required compression to the signal.

The expander has the input signal fed through the variable gain cell and then on to the output via the operational amplifier. The latter just acts as a buffer amplifier having fixed voltage gain in this case. The precision rectifier is fed with the input signal, and the higher the input signal, the greater the gain of the variable gain cell. This gives the required expansion effect, and provided the compressor and expander circuits are properly matched, the overall gain of the system is constant over a wide range of signal levels. Having the expander and compressor circuits based on what are essentially the same basic circuit blocks ensures that good matching is obtained.

The compressor and expander circuits are shown in Figures 2.13 and 2.14 respectively. As will be apparent from these, few discrete components are required. These are mostly input and output coupling capacitors, and bias resistors in the cases of R1 and R2. C3 and C10 are smoothing capacitors in the precision rectifier circuits. These must have the same values so that the attack/decay times of the expander match those of the compressor. C4 is needed in order to aid good stability. Note that with the compander fitted, the polarity of C13 in the main delay line circuit should be reversed (i.e. its positive terminal should connect to pin 10 of the NE570/NE571, and its negative terminal should connect to R7 etc. in the delay line). Obviously SK2 is moved to the input of the compressor and SK1 is moved to the output of the expander.

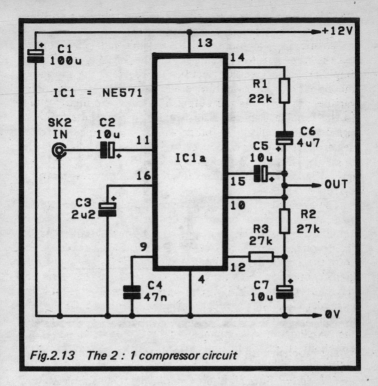

Fig.2.13 *The 2 : 1 compressor circuit*

It is possible to obtain improved distortion performance from the NE570 and NE571 by including a simple trimming circuit (Figure 2.15). Note that the compressor and expander require separate distortion trimming circuits, one feeding into pin 9 (compressor) and the other feeding into pin 8 (expander). Without a distortion trimming control the distortion level is a maximum of 1% for the NE570, and 2% for the NE571. However, the typical distortion levels are only 0.3% and 0.5% respectively, and many devices will have distortion levels significantly lower than these figures. Including the distortion trimming controls might not give any significant improvement in the overall performance of the system, particularly if you use the NE570.

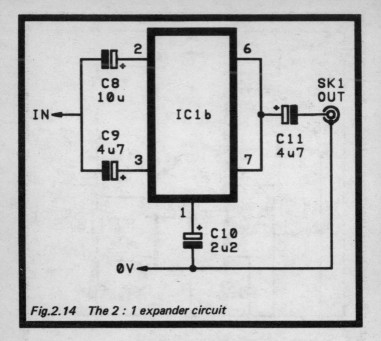

Fig.2.14   The 2 : 1 expander circuit

The problem with including the distortion trimming control is that it is difficult to set it up accurately without the aid of some fairly sophisticated test equipment. One simple way of adjusting these controls is to feed a sinewave signal at about 500Hz into the system, and then adjust them for optimum results "by ear". However, you will need a keen sense of hearing in order to obtain optimum results in this way. You will also need to feed the output of the expander or compressor into a reasonably good quality audio system. Probably the best option in the absence of distortion measuring equipment is to omit the distortion trimming controls and to use an NE570 for IC1.

One slight problem when incorporating the compander into the delay line is that it requires a supply potential of about 12 volts, but the rest of the unit operates from a 5 volt supply. The mains power supply circuit described previously only provides a 5 volt output. Probably the easiest solution is to

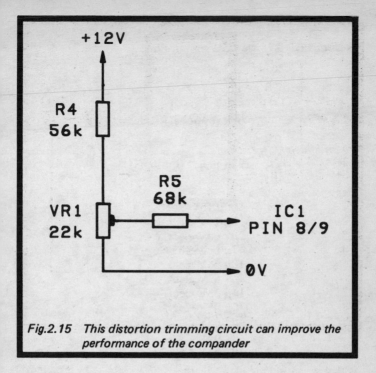

*Fig.2.15   This distortion trimming circuit can improve the
performance of the compander*

power the compander from the mains power supply unit, but
taking the positive supply from ahead of the stabiliser. In
other words, take the positive supply for the compander from
C1+ in the mains power supply. This will give a suitable
supply voltage, and the high value of C1 ensures that the
supply here is reasonably free from ripple. The current
consumption of the compander circuit is 4 milliamps at most
incidentally (3.2 milliamps typical).

Although the unit has been described here as a mono delay
line, it is quite easy to build a stereo version. It is just a matter
of building two units, one for each stereo channel. The mains
power supply is quite capable of powering two delay line
circuits.

Components for Compander (Figs 2.13, 2.14 and 2.15)

Resistors (all 0.25 watt 5% carbon film)
R1	22k
R2	27k
R3	27k
R4	56k (optional)
R5	68k (optional)

Potentiometer
VR1	22k preset (optional)

Capacitors
C1	100μ 16V elect
C2	10μ 25V elect
C3	2μ2 63V elect
C4	47n polyester
C5	10μ 25V elect
C6	4μ7 63V elect
C7	10μ 25V elect
C8	10μ 25V elect
C9	4μ7 63V elect
C10	2μ2 63V elect
C11	4μ7 63V elect

Semiconductor
IC1	NE570 or NE571 (see text)

Miscellaneous
SK1	Standard ¼ inch jack socket

Echo Effect

Delay lines can be used as signal processors for something like delay equalisation in a public address system, but they are more normally used with some additional circuitry to provide effects such as echo and chorus. The two basic types of echo unit and the way in which these effects are obtained was discussed in Chapter 1. All that is really needed is a mixer circuit at the output in order to obtain a single echo,

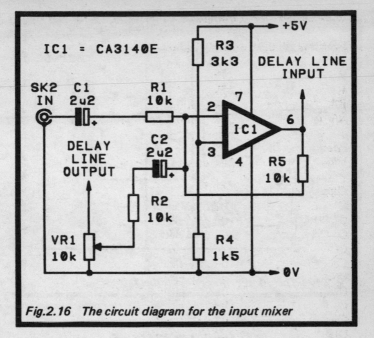

Fig.2.16 The circuit diagram for the input mixer

or a mixer at the input if a multiple (fading) echo effect is required.

Suitable mixer circuits for both types of echo effect are provided here. The input mixer circuit appears in Figure 2.16 while the output mixer circuit is shown in Figure 2.17. These are both simple summing mode mixers of conventional design. In the case of the input mixer VR1 controls the amount of feedback, and therefore determines how many times each sound is repeated before it decays to an insignificant level. Avoid setting the feedback level so high that signals are circulated indefinitely so that the signal level builds up to the point where overloading occurs. With the output mixer the level of the delayed signal is controlled by VR1, and it effectively sets the echo's volume. There is no feedback in this case and no danger of the signal level building up and causing overloads.

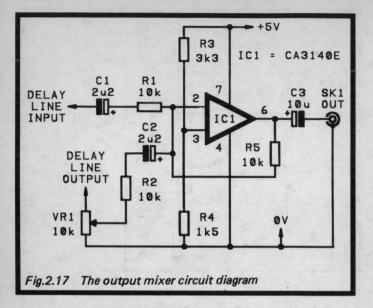

Fig.2.17 The output mixer circuit diagram

Components for Input Mixer (Fig. 2.16)

Resistors (all 0.25 watt 5% carbon film)
R1	10k
R2	10k
R3	3k3
R4	1k5
R5	10k

Potentiometer
VR1	10k log

Capacitors
C1	2μ2 63V elect
C2	2μ2 63V elect

Semiconductor
IC1	CA3140E

Miscellaneous
SK2   Standard ¼ inch jack socket

Components for Output Mixer (Fig. 2.17)

Resistors (all 0.25 watt 5% carbon film)
R1   10k
R2   10k
R3   3k3
R4   1k5
R5   10k

Potentiometer
VR1   10k log

Capacitors
C1 $2\mu2$ 63V elect
C2 $2\mu2$ 63V elect
C3 10μ 25V elect

Semiconductor
IC1   CA3140E

Miscellaneous
SK1   Standard ¼ inch jack socket

More Memory
For most purposes 8k of memory will be sufficient. If you
should wish to obtain a fairly long delay time, one possibility
is to slow down the sampling rate by using a higher value
for C1 in the clock generator circuit. The cutoff frequency
of the input and output filters would then need to be
reduced, and this will give less than the full audio bandwidth
from the system. A better way of increasing the maximum
delay time is to add another RAM chip, giving 16k of memory
and doubling the maximum delay time. This is not too difficult to achieve as the 6264 RAM chips have enable inputs that
render any external address decoding unnecessary, and the

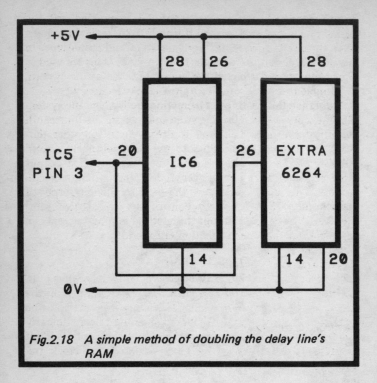

*Fig.2.18 A simple method of doubling the delay line's
RAM*

binary counter circuit has a fourteenth output that can be
used to control the additional RAM.

Figure 2.18 shows the basic method used. The additional
RAM chip is connected in exactly the same manner as the
original, except that its negative chip enable input (pin 20) is
fed from the binary counter instead of being tied to the
negative supply rail. The original RAM chip is connected in
the same manner as the original one except that its positive
chip enable input (pin 26) is driven from the binary counter
rather than being connected to the positive supply rail. The
result of this is that the first 8192 samples are written into
the original RAM chip which is activated by the fourteenth
output of the binary counter (which will be at logic 0). The
second RAM chip is disabled during this period. After 8192
samples have been taken, the fourteenth output of the binary

counter goes high, the original RAM chip is disabled, and the second one is enabled. After a further 8192 samples have been taken the circuit reverts to its original state, and it continues in this manner indefinitely. Thus the two RAM chips are used in turn, giving 16384 samples per complete cycle of the system, and double the delay time for a given clock frequency.

Note that this method of increasing the RAM in the system will not work with the scope store unit, where the fourteenth output of the binary counter is already used for other purposes. It should be possible to use this method if a third 4024BE is added to the counter circuit, with its first output being used to drive the trigger circuit and synchronisation output. This would then leave the most significant output of the second 4024BE free to control the two RAM chips. However, I have not tried out this method in practice, and can not guarantee that it will function satisfactorily.

Shorter Delays

Some effects do not require particularly long delay times. In fact for flanging and chorus effects the delay time of the circuit using 8k of RAM might be excessive even at the maximum clock frequency. Obtaining reduced delay times by using a higher clock frequency is not practical — the circuit simply will not function at substantially higher clock frequencies. The delay time can only be shortened by using less RAM.

Rather than changing to a smaller static RAM chip it is probably easier to simply use only part of the 6264's 8k of RAM. This is quite easily done, and it is basically just a matter of not connecting one or more of the most significant address lines to the binary counter circuit. Instead the line or lines concerned should simply be connected to the 0 volt supply rail. For example, disconnecting pin 2 of IC6 from IC5 and connecting it to the 0 volt rail will reduce the effective RAM of the system to 4k. Doing the same thing with pin 3 of IC6 as well reduces effective RAM to 2k, and giving pin 4 the same treatment gives just 1k of operational RAM.

1k of RAM should be about right for chorus effects. This effect is obtained by using an input mixer (such as the circuit described previously) to combine the delayed and non-delayed signal. It is very much like a single echo unit but with the delay time much lower at around 10 to 60 milliseconds. In this basic form the effect is really a "dual tracking" type, where a single voice (or whatever) fed into the input gives what sounds like two voices in unison at the output. A proper chorus effect requires the delay time to be varied so that a richer effect is obtained.

This can easily be achieved with this delay line circuit as the 555 timer used in the clock generator has a pin which can be used for this purpose. In normal (oscillator) operation the timing capacitor charges to two-thirds of the supply potential, then discharges to one-third of the supply voltage, then charges to two-thirds of the supply voltage again, and so on. Pin 5 of the device gives access to the potential divider circuit that sets the 2/3 V+ threshold level, and an external voltage applied to this pin can be used to pull this threshold level higher or lower in voltage. Taking it higher in voltage results in a longer charge/discharge time, and hence a lower output frequency. Reducing this threshold voltage has the opposite effect. The charge and discharge times are reduced, giving a higher output frequency.

Figure 2.19 shows the circuit for a low frequency oscillator that can be used to modulate the 555 clock generator so as to give an improved chorus effect. This is a conventional square/triangular oscillator of the type which uses a Miller Integrator (IC1a) and a Schmitt Trigger (IC1b). In this case it is the triangular output waveform from IC1a that is required. VR1 enables the modulation frequency to be varied from about 0.2Hz at maximum resistance (one cycle every five seconds) to about 6Hz at minimum resistance. VR2 permits the modulation depth to be varied, and S1 can be used to switch out the modulation altogether if desired.

If the flanging effect is required, use the delay line with about 1k of effective RAM and the input mixer circuit included so that feedback is obtained. Flanging is most effective when swept at a fairly low frequency, and so the low frequency modulation oscillator should be included in the unit. Using just the delay line plus low frequency modulation of the clock gives the vibrato effect (i.e. it gives frequency modulation of the input signal).

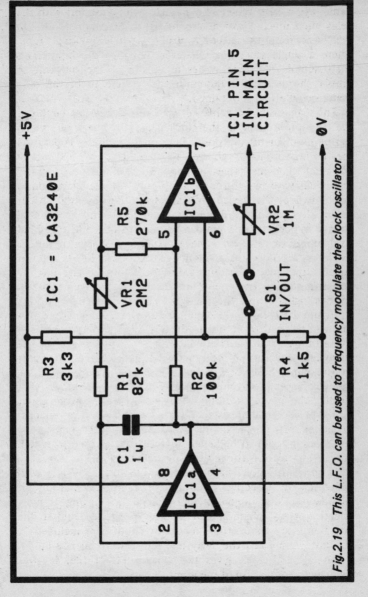

Fig.2.19 This L.F.O. can be used to frequency modulate the clock oscillator

79

Components for Low Frequency Oscillator (Fig. 2.19)

Resistors (all 0.25 watt 5% carbon film)
R1	82k
R2	100k
R3	3k3
R4	1k5
R5	270k

Potentiometers
VR1	2M2 lin
VR2	1M lin

Capacitor
C1	1μ polyester

Semiconductor
IC1	CA3240E

Miscellaneous
S1	SPST toggle

Finally
The circuits featured here provide plenty of scope for the experimenter, plus tried and tested circuits for those who simply wish to construct a digital echo unit, chorus unit, etc. Pinout and leadout diagram for the semcionductors used in these circuits are provided in Figure 2.20. Bear in mind that virtually all the integrated circuits used in these projects are MOS types, and that they consequently require the usual anti-static handling precautions to be observed. The Ferranti converter chips are bipolar devices, but as they are not particularly cheap they should still be treated with due respect. I would strongly urge the use of holders for all the d.i.l. integrated circuits.

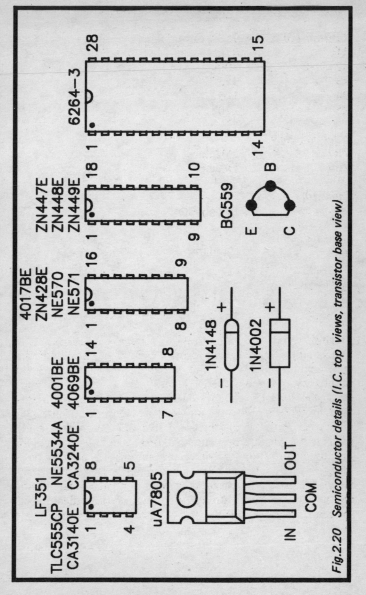

Fig.2.20 Semiconductor details (I.C. top views, transistor base view)

81

Notes

Notes

Notes

Please note following is a list of other titles that are available in our range of Radio, Electronics and Computer books.

These should be available from all good Booksellers, Radio Components Dealers and Mail Order Companies.

However, should you experience difficulty in obtaining any title in your area, then please write directly to the Publisher enclosing payment to cover the cost of the book plus adequate postage.

If you would like a complete catalogue of our entire range of Radio, Electronics and Computer books then please send a Stamped Addressed Envelope to:—

BERNARD BABANI (publishing) LTD
THE GRAMPIANS
SHEPHERDS BUSH ROAD
LONDON W6 7NF
ENGLAND